Entrepreneurship

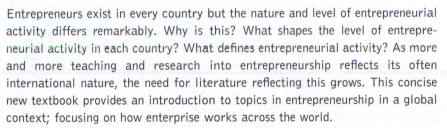

Entrepreneurs exist in every country but the nature and level of entrepreneurial activity differs remarkably. Why is this? What shapes the level of entrepreneurial activity in each country? What defines entrepreneurial activity? As more and more teaching and research into entrepreneurship reflects its often international nature, the need for literature reflecting this grows. This concise new textbook provides an introduction to topics in entrepreneurship in a global context; focusing on how enterprise works across the world.

Important topics such as financing, innovation and (anti)social enterprise are discussed in detail throughout the text, and examples and case studies are used to illustrate the application of different theoretical and conceptual approaches to entrepreneurship and the role it plays in developed, emerging and transitional economies.

Entrepreneurship: a global perspective is suitable for both final year undergraduate and postgraduate courses in enterprise and is likely to appeal particularly to student groups with a strong international element.

Stephen Roper is Professor of Enterprise at Warwick Business School, UK. Stephen has published widely in the areas of small business, innovation studies and entrepreneurship policy with recent papers in *Small Business Economics*, *Research Policy*, *International Small Business Journal* and *Environment and Planning A*. He is a consulting editor of the *International Small Business Journal* and works regularly with the OECD on SME policy development

ROUTLEDGE-ISBE MASTERS IN ENTREPRENEURSHIP

Edited by Colette Henry and Susan Marlow

The **Routledge-ISBE Masters in Entrepreneurship** series offers postgraduate students specialist but accessible textbooks on a range of entrepreneurship topics. Collectively, these texts form a significant resource base for those studying entrepreneurship, whether as part of an entrepreneurship-related programme of study, or as a new, non-cognate area for students in disciplines such as science and engineering, helping them to gain an in-depth understanding of contemporary entrepreneurial concepts.

The volumes in this series are authored by leading specialists in their field, and although they are discrete texts in their treatment of individual topics, all are united by a common structure and pedagogical approach. Key features of each volume include:

- A critical approach to combining theory with practice, which educates its reader rather than solely teaching a set of skills
- Clear learning objectives for each chapter
- The use of figures, tables and boxes to highlight key ideas, concepts and skills
- An annotated bibliography, guiding students in their further reading
- Discussion questions for each chapter to aid learning and put key concepts into practice

Entrepreneurship: a global perspective
Stephen Roper

Entrepreneurship

A global perspective

Stephen Roper

Routledge
Taylor & Francis Group

LONDON AND NEW YORK

First published 2013
by Routledge
2 Park Square, Milton Park, Abingdon, Oxon OX14 4RN

Simultaneously published in the USA and Canada
by Routledge
711 Third Avenue, New York, NY 10017

Routledge is an imprint of the Taylor & Francis Group, an informa business

British Library Cataloguing in Publication Data
A catalogue record for this book is available from the British Library

Library of Congress Cataloging in Publication Data
Roper, Stephen, 1960–
Entrepreneurship: a global perspective/Stephen Roper.
    p. cm. – (Routledge-ISBE masters in entrepreneurship)
    Includes bibliographical references and index.
    1. Entrepreneurship. 2. Entrepreneurship—Cross-cultural studies. I. Title.
    HB615.R65 2012
    338'.04—dc23
    2012004441

ISBN: 978-0-415-69552-7 (hbk)
ISBN: 978-0-415-69553-4 (pbk)
ISBN: 978-0-203-10435-4 (ebk)

Typeset in Perpetua and Bell Gothic
by Florence Production Ltd, Stoodleigh, Devon

Printed and bound in Great Britain by
TJ International Ltd, Padstow, Cornwall

Contents

Figures, tables and boxes

FIGURES

TABLES

BOXES

Series editors' foreword

ENTREPRENEURSHIP: A GLOBAL PHENOMENON

Entrepreneurial activities have fundamentally shaped human endeavour throughout history. However, since the 1980s, the phenomenon of entrepreneurship has re-emerged as a critical force in global economic development and wealth creation. In addition, the small and medium sized enterprise sector is now recognized as the most important source of new employment creation in all economies throughout the world. Thus, whilst entrepreneurship is feted as absolutely vital to fuel innovation, wealth generation and new employment, this 'umbrella' term covers a wide and diverse range of constructs, activities, policies and practices. Consequently, part of the attraction of studying entrepreneurship is the sheer diversity of the construct, which supports an endlessly fascinating multi-disciplinary critique.

As editors of this series, our aim is to encourage discussion and engagement with such conceptual and empirical diversity, but equally, we recognize that to enter the debate it is essential to offer an informed, multi-contextual perspective of entrepreneurship. As such, we are delighted to welcome the first book within this series – *Entrepreneurship: a global perspective*. In this, the inaugural volume in the series, Stephen Roper offers valuable but accessible insights into key issues informing the contemporary understanding of entrepreneurship. As an introductory text, it draws on current themes as well as recent empirical research but assumes no prior knowledge of entrepreneurship on the part of the student. Roper sets the scene for his text by explaining that entrepreneurial activity, which differs markedly between economies and individuals, can take many different forms around the globe. Essentially, entrepreneurship is a social process, influenced and conditioned by culture, economic conditions and regulatory frameworks. Thus, it needs to be understood at the global, as well as the national, regional and local levels. With this in mind, drawing on GEM (Global Entrepreneurship Monitor) data, Roper discusses the various national and international drivers of entrepreneurship, alongside the economic implications of entrepreneurship in higher- versus lower-income countries. The characteristics of successful entrepreneurs, and the various behavioural and cognitive perspectives on entrepreneurship are explained in the text before exploring business start-up decisions, processes and strategies. Small firm financing, innovation and social enterprise are other key areas covered in this volume. Again, such concepts are discussed in an international context, platforming the global nature of the entrepreneurial phenomenon. The book concludes by exploring enterprise policy, alongside the various drivers for and nature of government intervention in different economies. The fundamental question of how intervention should occur and how it should be evaluated is a final point of reflection for the reader.

The aim of this series is to provide a comprehensive overview of the main perspectives on entrepreneurship. The series explores the main approaches to entrepreneurship, as well as the various contexts in which it occurs. The rationale for the series is that we cannot understand entrepreneurship sufficiently, nor engage effectively in related contemporary debates, without an understanding of the key theories and concepts that underpin the field. As such, future texts within this series will seek to explore the multi-faceted nature of entrepreneurship as an evolving but truly global phenomenon.

Colette Henry and Susan Marlow, February 2012.

Preface

This book introduces students to the variety of entrepreneurship. It draws heavily on recent academic and statistical research, particularly from the Global Entrepreneurship Monitor project, the World Bank and the OECD. These studies provide valuable insights into national differences in the patterns of entrepreneurial activity. Company and thematic case studies are then used to illustrate the challenges faced by specific entrepreneurs and policy-makers in different countries. The case studies emphasize the importance of the individual in the entrepreneurship story and the combination of determination, self-confidence and ambition which characterizes many successful entrepreneurs. They also emphasize, however, the socially embedded nature of entrepreneurial activity and consequently the importance of the business and social environment within which entrepreneurs operate. In some more developed economies, such institutions are relatively stable. In other developing and transition economies institutions are altering rapidly, changing the context for entrepreneurship and, in turn, being changed by entrepreneurship. A neo-institutionalist perspective proves useful in linking changing institutions, individual agency and the interplay between the two.

Initial chapters in the book focus on the context for entrepreneurship and the global landscape of entrepreneurial activity. Subsequent chapters reflect the entrepreneurship journey focusing on the person of the entrepreneur, the start-up decision and the factors which determine business success. Later chapters focus on cross-cutting themes from the entrepreneurship literature – finance, innovation, antisocial enterprise and entrepreneurship policy. Insightful academic studies exist relating to each chapter: however, the vast majority of these remain single country studies and comparative studies of entrepreneurship remain relatively uncommon. Data difficulties clearly limit the scope of such studies but there remains significant potential for comparative studies of entrepreneurship to challenge received conceptual frameworks and further explore the interplay between national institutions and individual entrepreneurs in different international settings. Hopefully the following pages may inspire further research of this type.

Acknowledgements

This book is based on an optional module which I developed and have taught at Warwick Business School, UK for the last four years. My thanks are due to the students who have taken the module and whose encouragement was the stimulus for this book being written. My thanks are due also to my colleagues in the Centre for Small and Medium Enterprises at Warwick Business School for providing inspiration and distraction in appropriate measure during the writing process. Jim Love (Aston) and Nola Hewitt-Dundas (Queens, Belfast) proved more tolerant research collaborators than anyone has a right to expect. Finally, my thanks to my family – Marj, Amy and Anna – who now know more about global entrepreneurship than they ever wanted to know.

Chapter 1

Setting the scene

1.1 INTRODUCTION

Entrepreneurship exists everywhere because, as Bolton and Thompson (2000, p. 96) suggest, entrepreneurial opportunities

> can be found everywhere. Some are genuinely new; others are innovatory improvements on a theme. Some are limited growth ideas; others can be used to build global businesses. They only succeed if they are different in some meaningful way and executed effectively. There is, then, an infinite set of possibilities for people with the talent and temperament to become successful entrepreneurs to choose from.

But, as we shall see, the nature and focus of entrepreneurial activity differs markedly between countries and individuals. Some entrepreneurs seek to start 'born global' enterprises addressing an international market opportunity. In other less auspicious situations, entrepreneurship may be a matter of necessity. For some, entrepreneurship means creating a socially responsible business which complies with national legislation; for others, it may mean setting up a criminal enterprise network designed to traffic drugs or people.

A key objective of this book is to explore 'why' these differences in entrepreneurial activity emerge and to explore the consequences of national differences in entrepreneurial activity for a nation's economic and social development. Two key themes emerge. First, understanding differences in entrepreneurial activity requires a strongly contextual approach. Entrepreneurship is a social process which is strongly conditioned by local factors as well as a nation's contrasting cultures, economic conditions and legal and regulatory frameworks. For example, the technological profile of business opportunities differs markedly between countries, as does the availability of finance, market information and energy. How do these factors influence the nature of entrepreneurship activity? In conceptual terms, this suggests the potential value of an institutional approach which identifies separately the role of institutions (structure) and individual (agency) in shaping entrepreneurial decisions (North, 1990). In fact, the conceptual approach we adopt is neo-institutionalist, reflecting the potential for entrepreneurial activity itself to change the institutional environment in a country or countries (Tracey, 2011). McDade and Spring (2005), for example, describe networks of 'new generation' African entrepreneurs who have – to a greater or lesser extent – changed the environment for business in the countries in which they operate. The basis of a neo-institutionalist approach is outlined in more detail in Section 1.2.

The second theme to emerge from our analysis is the inadequacy – or perhaps more accurately, the irrelevance – of many of the standard taught 'models' of entrepreneurial behaviour for many countries. In particular, a study of comparative entrepreneurship rapidly exposes the assumptions implicit in many models which limit their generalizability. For example, consider the notion of the 'debt-tax' shield which it is argued may shape the financing preferences of entrepreneurs towards holding debt (see Chapter 7). What assumptions are implicit here? First, that the firm has a choice of financing options. Second, that the entrepreneur regards both debt and equity as ethically acceptable, and third, that the firm is in a situation where it is actually engaging with a tax system. For developed economies in Europe or North America these assumptions may be reasonable but for firms in many developing or transition economies, particularly those where there may be a preference for Islamic banking, they pose more difficulties and limit the generalizability of the notion of the debt-tax shield. Essentially similar considerations also relate the discussion of a financial pecking order and a number of other standard frameworks discussed in later chapters.

1.2 ENTREPRENEURSHIP IN CONTEXT

Institutional theory provides a useful framework for examining entrepreneurial behaviour in specific local contexts and the impact of national institutions on economic and social development (Tracey, 2011). The types of institutions considered as having an impact on economic activity relate not just to regulatory structures and legislative frameworks, but also include social norms and values. To quote Bruton *et al.* (2009) 'regulatory structures include both laws and regulations generated by the government . . . in contrast the normative and cognitive institutional pillars are socially constructed over time, and come to be perceived as the natural and factual order' (p. 765). A nation's institutional profile may either restrict the opportunities available to individuals or enterprises or create opportunities for entrepreneurial activity. For example, Djankov *et al.* (2002b) use data collected by the World Bank to compare the impact of regulatory structures on business start-ups in 85 countries. This data describes significant international differences in the number of procedures which potential entrepreneurs have to undertake to start a firm and the cost of these procedures. It is suggested that these institutional differences may make a significant difference to the profile of business start-ups between countries as well as having implications for levels of corruption etc.

Institutional models, therefore, suggest that entrepreneurial behaviour will be shaped in part as a response to institutional structures. Discussing the nature of different types of institutions North (1990, p. 6) suggests, however, that 'although formal rules may change overnight as the result of political and judicial decisions, informal constraints embodied in culture, custom, tradition and codes of conduct are much more impervious to deliberate policies'. More recent developments in institutional theory have, however, questioned the stability of institutions in some international contexts. Bruton *et al.* (2009, p. 775), for example, suggest that drawing largely on the historical development of European and North American economies

> institutions are viewed as static and only changing very slowly over time . . . in the fast-changing environment of emerging economies, new institutions are developing and actors in the environment can shape existing institutions. These new institutions are evolving to meet the shift to a market orientation and the increasing economic activity.

The potential for new and rapidly developing institutions suggests, Bruton *et al.* (2009) argue, a need for a more flexible approach to extend the application of institutional analysis into developing and emerging economies and to encompass developments in new or emerging industries. In the dynamic context of the US wind energy sector, for example, Sine and Lee (2009, p. 152) emphasize that entrepreneurship is 'substantively different' to that in a more stable institutional environment. In particular, while they argue that existing institutions may be less conducive to entrepreneurship due to the 'low cognitive and socio-political legitimacy' of entrepreneurship it remains the case that

> the processes of opportunity creation and discovery as well as the proclivities of entrepreneurs are actively shaped by powerful institutional actors. The creation of institutional infrastructures, norms, values, cognitive frameworks and regulations create value for, and give purpose to, entrepreneurial activity.

The need to allow for institutional change, and for the possibility of a range of different entrepreneurial responses – either individual or corporate – to a common institutional environment, has led to the development of neo-institutionalist perspectives. Here, individuals' entrepreneurial response to their institutional setting is said to be shaped by the extent and nature of their embeddedness within their societal and organizational contexts. For example, firms undertaking inward investment with few pre-existing links to a new geographic market may introduce new business models. Existing firms, more strongly embedded within local market

3

structures and network relations, may find the same innovation difficult (Kostova, 1999). This suggests the potential for diverse entrepreneurial responses to a given set of institutional conditions and the potential for entrepreneurial acts – or acts of corporate venturing – to influence existing institutional structures or create new institutions (Tracey, 2011).

1.3 OUTLINE OF LATER CHAPTERS

The remainder of the book is divided into three main sections. The first section comprises Chapters 2 and 3 and focuses on contrasts in the global context for entrepreneurial activity. Chapter 2 focuses on the combination of global and local conditions – the institutional context – within which entrepreneurship occurs in different countries. A key focus is the idea of the entrepreneurial regional innovation system developed by Cooke and Leydesdorff (2006). Data from the Global Entrepreneurship Monitor or GEM project is used to highlight international contrasts in the level of entrepreneurial activity. Chapter 3 focuses on the social and economic development implications of entrepreneurial activity, emphasizing the contribution of entrepreneurship to job growth, technological development and social cohesion. The experience of contrasting countries, however, suggests that these beneficial effects of entrepreneurial activity cannot be assumed.

The second section of the book comprising Chapters 4, 5 and 6 focuses on a comparative analysis of aspects of the entrepreneurial journey. Chapter 4 focuses on the person of the entrepreneur. What factors characterize an entrepreneur? How are these factors related to the institutional context within which the entrepreneur is operating? Chapter 5 focuses on the start-up decision and considers the value of economic, social and process perspectives. Chapter 6 then examines the factors which influence business success. Perhaps the key points here are the relative weakness of existing models in explaining the diversity of firm growth rates and the potential role of factors such as luck in explaining growth (Parnell and Dent, 2009).

The final section of the book comprising Chapters 7 to 10 focuses on a series of cross-cutting issues which emerge from the research literature. Chapter 7, for example, focuses on business finance, reflecting contrasts in funding preferences and priorities in different countries. A specific focus of attention in this chapter is Islamic finance and its potential value in supporting entrepreneurial activity. Chapter 8 focuses on innovation in smaller firms, a discussion which links back to the notion of the entrepreneurial regional innovation system discussed in Chapter 2. Chapter 9 then focuses on criminal or antisocial enterprise. This is an important issue in its own right but it also sheds light on the moral content of 'entrepreneurship' itself. Chapter 10 focuses on entrepreneurship policy and its strongly contingent role in supporting enterprise development. This chapter also considers issues of policy evaluation.

Chapter 2

A world of enterprise

2.1 INTRODUCTION

While entrepreneurs are found in every country in the world, the opportunities they face and the institutions which influence their activities differ greatly. In this chapter we focus on the interaction of global factors – linked, for example, to technological change, global supply chains, international trade agreements, etc. – and local factors in shaping the institutional environment for entrepreneurship. Elizabeth Chell called this 'glocalization', meaning that

> given increased pressures to globalize, standards of performance need to be matched at that level if the company is to hold its own. Offering products and services which can compete globally will also assure success in local markets. In this way, it may be argued that companies can be both globally and locally competitive: they can be 'glocal'.
>
> (Chell, 2001, p. 51)

Of course, the need to be glocal differs greatly depending on context; street traders in developing economies are more strongly influenced by local rather than global factors, while the opportunities for a 'born global' or technology-based start-up will be more strongly influenced by global market conditions (Efrat and Shoham, 2011).

Different perspectives exist on the key factors which are shaping the global economy, and the global environment for entrepreneurship. Some researchers have emphasized international contrasts in governance and alternative 'modes of capitalism', identifying commonalities between countries on the basis of their governance profiles. In particular, contrasts are often drawn between the more laissez-faire, Anglo-Saxon mode of capitalism of the USA and the traditions of Rhenish capitalism in countries such as Germany and Austria (Green et al., 2010). Other academics have focused on global supply networks or supply chains, viewing changes in the international economy through the changing power of suppliers and

5

buyers (Ernst and Kim, 2002, Henderson *et al.*, 2002). In either view, the growth of the BRIC countries – Brazil, Russia, India and China – and other developing economies is rapidly changing the global economic landscape and reshaping the global set of entrepreneurial opportunities. Increasingly, these changes mean that innovation-based competition is replacing cost-based competition, reflecting Baumol's comment that

> firms cannot afford to leave innovation to chance. Rather, managements are forced by market pressures to support innovation activity systematically . . . The result is a ferocious arms race among firms in the most rapidly evolving sectors of the economy, with innovation as the prime weapon.
>
> (Baumol, 2002, p. ix)

This is not just an issue for company leaders, however, as policy-makers in different countries – and supra-national bodies such as the European Union – invest in R&D and innovation in an attempt to develop national competitiveness and productivity (Guellec and von Pottelsberghe, 2001, 2004).

Pressure to compete through innovation also has implications for the 'local', potentially changing the spatial distribution of economic activity as entrepreneurs search for competitive advantage. International attention on the 'local' factors which influence entrepreneurship and competitiveness has often focused on technological hot-spots such as Silicon Valley (Saxenian, 1996, Bresnahan and Gambardella, 2004). Perspectives from new economic geography are also relevant here, however, suggesting that the spatial distribution of economic activity may reflect the balance between agglomeration advantages and transportation costs (Fujita and Thisse, 2002). A desire to avoid local competition, the search for lower production cost, and costs of transportation may encourage geographic dispersion; while positive Marshallian externalities and informational advantages may encourage spatial agglomeration and clustering (Koski *et al.*, 2002). Arguably, however, global moves towards innovation-based competition, accompanied by the rapid development of connectivity and global logistics, have radically shifted the historical balance between these centralizing and de-centralizing forces. On one hand, the increasing importance of innovation as the basis for competitiveness may have strengthened the centralizing forces as 'knowledge spillovers tend to be spatially restricted . . . [this] has triggered a resurgence in the importance of local regions as a key source of comparative advantage' (Audretsch, 1998, p. 26). On the other hand, improved connectivity and global logistics might encourage the dispersal of commercial and industrial activity, and the geographical separation of elements of the development and production process. For example, the increasing globalization of R&D activity may mean that the spatial distribution of the commercial benefits of R&D activity may be very different to that of the R&D activity itself (Reddy, 1997).

Discussion of both the 'local' and 'global' emphasize the importance of the institutional environment in which entrepreneurship takes place. This discussion also emphasizes the dynamic – rather than the static – nature of many of the institutions which influence entrepreneurial activity (Tracey, 2011). In the next sections we therefore dwell briefly on three alternative theoretical perspectives on the institutional factors which shape entrepreneurship and international competitiveness at different levels of analysis. To reflect the local dimension we focus first on the literature on entrepreneurial regional innovation systems. To reflect contrasts at national level we explore the literature on varieties of capitalism, and to reflect the international dimension that of global supply networks and supply chains. Following this, we introduce some of the key data sources which provide an indication of contrasting levels of entrepreneurship and start-up activity across the globe. Specifically, we focus on data from the Global Entrepreneurship Monitor (or GEM) project and the OECD. What do these tell us about the global distribution of enterprise activity?

The learning objectives for this chapter are as follows:

- To introduce students to the main conceptual frameworks which have been used to reflect the different national and international contexts within which entrepreneurship occurs.
- To introduce students to the global landscape of entrepreneurial activity and some of the key international indicators.
- To make students aware of some of the potential explanations for international variations in the level and nature of entrepreneurial activity.

Further reading and discussion questions are included in Section 2.5.

2.2 LOCAL, NATIONAL AND INTERNATIONAL DRIVERS OF ENTREPRENEURSHIP

In the literature on business innovation the notion of an 'innovation system' has a relatively long history, although the link to entrepreneurship is more recent (Cooke and Leydesdorff, 2006). Metcalfe (1997, pp. 461–2), for example, suggests an innovation system is

> . . . that set of distinct institutions which jointly and individually contribute to the development and diffusion of new technologies and which provides the framework within which governments form and implement policies to influence the innovation process. As such it is a system of interconnected institutions to create, store and transfer the knowledge, skills and artefacts which define new technology.

7

Originally developed to reflect national differences in innovation performance (Nelson, 1993) more recent discussion has focused on regional innovation systems to reflect more local influences on innovation and entrepreneurial activity (Braczyk *et al.*, 1998, Cooke *et al.*, 1997, Cooke, 2004, Fuchs and Shapira, 2005). Some writers have emphasized the institutional and agglomeration advantages of particular locations (Cooke and Leydesdorff, 2006, Dolfsma and Leydesdorff, 2009) while others, such as Richard Florida, have focused on the ability of cities to attract talented and skilled residents (Florida, 2005).

The literature on innovation systems emphasizes the systemic nature of economic change and the importance of an evolutionary approach to understanding institutional development. Ylinenpaa (2009) contrasts this system-wide approach in the innovation literature and the focus of much entrepreneurship research on the individual, and highlights the distinction make by Cooke and Leydesdorff (2006) between institutional regional innovation systems (IRIS) and entrepreneurial regional innovation systems (ERIS). IRIS emphasize engineering-led innovation among existing firms based on close and enduring networks and which Cooke and Leydesdorff (2006) suggest are typical of Germany and the Nordic countries. In the alternative ERIS, which Cooke and Leydesdorff (2006) suggest are more representative of the Anglo-American economies, innovation is entrepreneurially led, relying more on the opportunistic actions of individuals and small firms than long-term partnerships between existing firms. More recent studies have emphasized entrepreneurial activity as one of the key functions of innovation systems. Suurs *et al.* (2010) in their discussion of the development of the natural gas innovation system in the Netherlands, for example, characterize the innovation system as having seven 'functions', of which one is Entrepreneurial Activity (Table 2.1). They argue that in the case they are considering, and others associated with the development of new innovation systems in new technologies or rapidly changing economic contexts, the entrepreneurial function is crucial to system development.

Suurs *et al.* (2010) also emphasize, however, the extent to which the opportunities for entrepreneurial activity are shaped by other ERIS functions. For example, they stress the impact of regulatory and legislative changes on creating new business opportunities, while others have stressed the role of public procurement, for example, as a means of stimulating entrepreneurship and innovation (Edler and Georghiou, 2007). In either case, the emphasis is on the local with the potential for regional, city or district governments to shape institutions to create new opportunities or incentives for entrepreneurial activity. Ylinenpaa (2009) provides an example of a local entrepreneurial innovation system based around a Swedish company called DesignTech (Box 2.1).

While discussion of entrepreneurial regional innovation systems has focused on local institutions and their capabilities and interaction, a complementary literature on varieties of capitalism has focused on different configurations of national

Table 2.1 *Innovation system functions*

Function 1. Entrepreneurial Activity – The core of the innovation system. Risk-takers exploit business opportunities and perform innovative and/or practice-oriented experiments.

Function 2. Knowledge Development – Technological R&D is the key source of variety in the system and one of the key building blocks for technological innovation.

Function 3. Knowledge Diffusion – The process through which knowledge is exchanged and diffused through networks and linkages between organizations.

Function 4. Guidance of the Innovation System – The process of selection through which variety is reduced and convergence in development is achieved.

Function 5. Market Formation – New market formulation to create opportunities for innovation. Could be the result of legislation, regulatory or entrepreneurial activity.

Function 6. Resource Mobilization – Financial, material and human factors are all necessary for innovation system development.

Function 7. Support from Advocacy Coalitions – Establishing legitimacy of innovations developed through the system.

Source: Adapted from Suurs *et al.*, 2010, Table 1, p. 421

BOX 2.1 DESIGNTECH'S INNOVATION SYSTEM

DesignTech is a small software company located in the Aurorum Science Park in Lulea, Sweden. Originally established in 2001, the company has its origins in Lulea University of Technology. DesignTech has established itself as the hub for a small regional innovation system comprising different types of organizations with different competencies: R&D competencies are represented by a contracted researcher at the university who functions as the firm's out-sourced unit for strategic product development; financing competencies are represented by local and regional venture capitalists who have supported the development of DesignTech's development. The engagement of the two owners of the company (its managing director and its sales/marketing manager) and one employee responsible for product development in the company have been crucial to the development of relationships and trust with external partners.

'The orientation towards individuals is also very visible when the company describes the innovation system it belongs to: it is individuals and their specific personalities who are important and not primarily the organizations or institutions they represent' (Ylinenpaa, 2009, p. 1162). The company continues this philosophy of partnering as a driver of growth: 'DesignTech believes that growth is fuelled by strong partners and is committed to building long-term, mutually sustaining relationships with its partners'.

Sources: Ylinenpaa (2009) and http://www.designtech.se

institutions. Chizema and Buck (2006), for example, argue that in terms of corporate governance it is possible to distinguish between countries marked by 'stock market capitalism' – typically the UK and the USA – and those marked by 'welfare capitalism' such as Germany, Austria, Japan and the Netherlands. Neither, they argue, is necessarily 'superior' but both are likely to be subject to substantial 'inertia' as 'dominant stakeholders may have the power to thwart attempts to introduce new institutions, to defend their own positions of power' (p. 491). Institutional frameworks which support 'welfare capitalism' in particular may be less conducive to entrepreneurial activity (Cooke and Leydesdorff, 2006, Bruton et al., 2009).

A common critique of the focus on national institutional frameworks, implicit in both of the innovation systems and varieties of capitalism literature is, however, that they over-emphasize the importance of local factors and underplay the impact of globalizing pressures. Attempts to overcome these difficulties have been made in the work by Ernst and Kim (2002) and Henderson et al. (2002) on the notions of global production chains or global production networks. Both have attempted to develop a conceptual framework to reflect the global, regional and local economic influences on economic activity. More specifically, Henderson et al. (2002), for example, suggest a definition of a global production network (GPN) as

> the global network of firms, institutions and other economic agents which shapes, and is shaped by: the fundamental processes of knowledge and wealth creation, enhancement and exploitation; corporate, collective and institutional elements of organizational power; and, spatial and network embeddedness.

The intention here is clear; on the one hand to recognize the importance of globalizing forces, and in particular the influence of multinational companies and international capital markets, while also encompassing the potential for significant local advantages and development trajectories.

> GPNs do not only connect firms functionally and territorially but also they connect aspects of the social and spatial arrangements in which those firms are embedded and which influence their strategies and the values, priorities and expectations of managers, workers and communities alike.
>
> (Henderson et al., 2002, p. 451)

2.3 A WORLD OF ENTERPRISE

As the earlier discussion suggests, local economic, social and cultural conditions, national regulatory and legislative factors and global production networks all point to very different profiles of enterprise activity in different countries. One of the most interesting data sources which provide this type of comparative data between countries is the Global Entrepreneurship Monitor or GEM project. This is an international research project which now includes research teams in more than 50 different countries each of which conduct surveys of the adult population to identify levels of participation in entrepreneurial activity. A key feature of the GEM international comparisons is a common definition of entrepreneurship. Specifically, in GEM a person is said to be engaged in entrepreneurship if they are involved in trying to start a new business or facilitate the expansion of an existing business. For statistical comparisons GEM defines a business as 'new' if it is less than 42 months old, with the main measure of a nation's entrepreneurship activity being the Total Entrepreneurial Activity rate or TEA rate. This is defined as:

$$\text{TEA rate} = \frac{\text{Number of adults engaged in entrepreneurship} \times 100}{\text{Total adult population}}$$

Results for the TEA rate for different countries are given in Table 2.2. Grouping countries into those in which economic growth is largely Factor-driven, Efficiency-driven and Innovation-driven provides a broad indication of how levels of entrepreneurial activity differ between stages of development as suggested by the World Economic Forum's Global Competitiveness Report. On average, in the group of Factor-driven developing economies, 22.8 per cent of the adult population were involved in enterprise activity, although this rose to 52.2 per cent in Vanuatu. In the Efficiency-driven group of transition and productivity-led econ-omies, an average of 11.8 per cent of the adult population was engaged in enterprise, almost twice the average of 5.6 per cent in the more developed, Innovation-driven, economies (Table 2.2). These differences in average TEA rates emphasize the impact of local economic, social and cultural conditions on levels of entrepreneurial activity but also emphasize the much greater homogeneity of levels of entrepreneurial activity among the Innovation-driven economies. Among the Factor-driven economies, the coefficient of variation of TEA rates, for example, was 0.64, compared to 0.52 for the Efficiency-driven economies and only 0.33 for the Innovation-driven economies. One possible interpretation is that levels of entrepreneurial activity in the Factor-driven economies are shaped more strongly by diverse local conditions; while levels of entrepreneurial activity in the Innovation-driven economies are shaped more strongly by more global factors linked to international trade or trade regulation.

Perhaps the most striking feature of Table 2.2, however, is the much higher level of entrepreneurial activity in the Factor-driven countries than in the Innovation-driven countries. This is perhaps surprising given the earlier discussion on entrepreneurial regional innovation systems which suggested that stronger ERIS might contribute to higher levels of entrepreneurial activity. Instead, this is not what we see, with levels of entrepreneurial activity actually higher in countries

Table 2.2 Total entrepreneurial activity, 2010

Factor-driven economies		Efficiency-driven economies		Innovation-driven economies	
Country	TEA %	Country	TEA %	Country	TEA %
Angola	32.4	Argentina	14.2	Australia	7.8
Bolivia	38.6	Bosnia and Herz.	7.7	Belgium	3.7
Egypt	7.0	Brazil	17.5	Denmark	3.8
Ghana	33.9	Chile	16.8	Finland	5.7
Guatemala	16.3	China	14.4	France	5.8
Iran	12.4	Colombia	20.6	Germany	4.2
Jamaica	10.5	Costa Rica	13.5	Greece	5.5
Pakistan	9.1	Croatia	5.5	Iceland	10.6
Saudi Arabia	9.4	Ecuador	21.3	Ireland	6.8
Uganda	31.3	Hungary	7.1	Israel	5.7
Vanuatu	52.2	Latvia	9.7	Italy	2.3
West Bank/Gaza Strip	10.4	Macedonia	8.0	Japan	3.3
Zambia	32.6	Malaysia	5.0	Republic of Korea	6.6
		Montenegro	14.9	Netherlands	7.2
		Peru	27.2	Norway	7.7
		Romania	4.3	Portugal	4.5
		Russia	3.9	Slovenia	4.7
		South Africa	8.9	Spain	4.3
		Taiwan	8.4	Sweden	4.9
		Trinidad and Tobago	15.1	Switzerland	5.0
		Tunisia	6.1	United Kingdom	6.4
		Turkey	8.6	United States	7.6
		Uruguay	11.7		
Average	22.8	Average	11.8	Average	5.6

Source: GEM Global Report 2010, Table 3, pp. 17–18. See: www.gemconsortium.org.

where we might have thought that the institutional framework for entrepreneurship might actually be weaker. So why is this the case? Well, two other statistics derived from the GEM data suggest part of the answer. GEM distinguishes between what is called 'opportunity-driven' and 'necessity-driven' entrepreneurship: opportunity-driven entrepreneurship is when entrepreneurs are pulled into entrepreneurship due to a market opportunity which may improve or maintain their incomes or increase their independence. Necessity-based entrepreneurship occurs when entrepreneurs are pushed into entrepreneurship because they need a source of income (Langan-Fox, 2005). On average in the Factor-driven economies the GEM Global Report 2010 suggests that 34 per cent of entrepreneurial activity was necessity-based compared to an average of 31 per cent in the Efficiency-driven economies and 20 per cent in the Innovation-driven economies. The implication is that necessity-based entrepreneurship is more important in the Factor-driven economies, although even here opportunity remains the dominant driver of entrepreneurial activity. Moreover, it is clear that the difference between the importance of necessity-based entrepreneurship in the Factor-driven and Innovation-driven economies cannot account for the whole difference in levels of entrepreneurial activity between the two groups of countries. Instead, the figures suggest that both the opportunities for entrepreneurship and the necessity for entrepreneurship are greater in the Factor-based economies than in the Innovation-driven economies.

While the GEM data provides much useful information on the prevalence of entrepreneurial activity it tells us little about the more general profile of start-up activity in different world economies. Here information from the OECD Entrepreneurship Indicators project is more useful and also provides some information on the survival of enterprises in different countries. In particular, for a smaller number of countries than covered by the GEM survey, the OECD data provides an indication of birth and death rates of enterprises. In the OECD figures a firm 'birth' relates to a new firm with at least one employee which has been established in the last year. Likewise a firm 'death' occurs when an enterprise with at least one employee closes. In each case birth and death rates are expressed as a percentage of the population of active enterprises with at least one employee. Among the countries considered – which are primarily in what GEM would categorize as Innovation-driven – the highest firm birth rates occurred in Portugal and Estonia, with notably lower rates in the USA and Israel (Figure 2.1). Death rates also vary widely between countries, with Denmark having relatively high and Norway relatively low firm death rates in 2005 (Figure 2.2). The correlation coefficient between firm birth and death rates is 0.465 suggesting also that countries with higher firm birth rates also tend to have higher firm death rates. Despite this the evidence is clear that across both low- and high-income countries firm start-up and the wider small business sector is a net contributor to employment growth (Ayyagari *et al.*, 2011)

One other issue suggested by the GEM data and other international sources is the under-representation of women in entrepreneurship in most countries. The 2007 GEM report 'Women in Enterprise', for example, focused on the ratio of the female to male TEA rates and suggested that in countries like Belgium the female TEA rate was only 23.7 per cent of that of males. In many other European countries the female TEA rate was also significantly less than half of that for males or, put another way, more than twice as many males were involved in entrepreneurship as females. Why is this? A number of different explanations have been suggested including cultural, educational and aspirational differences as well as differences in the access to financial and managerial resources of males and females (Lerner *et al.*, 1997). The under-representation of women in enterprise is not universal, however, and one exception is China, where the TEA rates for males and females were almost identical in 2007 (Box 2.2).

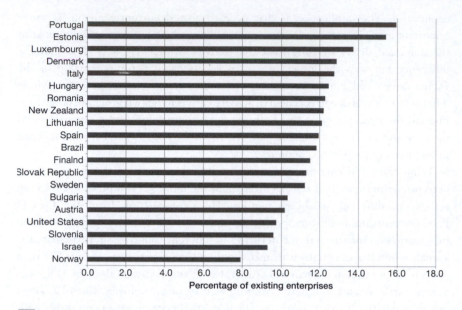

Figure 2.1
Firm birth rates in services – selected countries, 2006

Source: Measuring entrepreneurship 2009, OECD, Annex B.
See: www.oecd.org/statistics/measuringentrepreneurship.

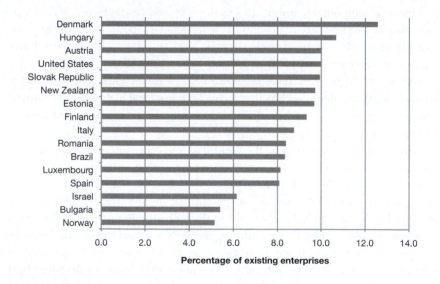

Figure 2.2
Firm death rates in services – selected countries, 2005

Source: Measuring entrepreneurship 2009, OECD, Annex B.
See: www.oecd.org/statistics/measuringentrepreneurship.

BOX 2.2 FEMALE ENTREPRENEURS IN CHINA AND GERMANY

Rosenbusch *et al.* compare the characteristics and success of female and male entrepreneurs in China and Germany selected from the car and machinery, software development, hotels and catering, and building industries. Their results suggest significant differences in the human capital and experience of male and female entrepreneurs in Germany but no such differences in China. In addition in Germany human capital effects on enterprise performance were also more significant than those in China. They concluded:

> We found that gender differences are more prevalent in Germany than in China. . . . The most important difference between male and female entrepreneurs occurred for managerial experience. First, women have significantly less managerial experience than men. However, this applies only to the German context. We attribute this finding to different role expectations in the two countries and a greater participation rate of women in the workforce in China.

Source: Rosenbusch *et al.* (2009)

2.4 SUMMARY AND KEY POINTS

Both theory and international data sources emphasize the extent to which entrepreneurship activity is contextual, influenced strongly by local and national institutional factors. Global markets and supply chains also play an important role in influencing the development of some types of enterprise, however, particularly those exposed to international market competition. Conceptual views of this combination of 'local' and 'global' factors vary, emphasizing the systemic character of local entrepreneurship systems, national institutional profiles and power relationships within global supply chains. One interpretation might be that levels of entrepreneurial activity might be expected to be greater in localities or countries where the network of institutions is better developed. In fact, however, international data sources tend to suggest that levels of entrepreneurial activity are higher in lower-income, Factor-driven economies rather than more highly developed Innovation-driven economies. In part this is linked to higher levels of necessity-based entrepreneurship in lower-income economies, but levels of opportunity-based entrepreneurship are also greater in many of these countries.

Two other regularities are suggested by international data comparisons. First, considering firm birth rates from a group of Innovation-driven economies suggests

15 ■

that in any year firm births are equivalent to around 8–15 per cent of the existing stock of enterprises. Firm deaths are broadly similar in scale, suggesting much smaller net changes in the stock of enterprises of perhaps 2–5 per cent. Second, with some notable exceptions – e.g. China – women are typically under-represented in entrepreneurship across the globe reflecting a varying mix of institutional influences. Both issues are considered in later chapters.

2.5 DISCUSSION QUESTIONS AND FURTHER READING

A more extensive discussion of the notion of glocalization can be found in Chapter 2 of the book by Elizabeth Chell (2001) called *Entrepreneurship: Globalization, innovation and development* . Cooke and Leydesdorff (2006) provide an accessible introduction to the literature on innovation systems while the paper by Henderson *et al.* (2002) provides a less accessible but very insightful introduction to global production networks. Michael Porter's (1998) paper in the *Harvard Business Review* – 'Clusters and the new economics of competition' – is also relevant to the issues addressed in this chapter.

A key data resource for this chapter – and indeed much of the rest of the book – is the group of country and international reports published by the GEM Consortium. These are available at: http://www.gemconsortium.org. Along with the national reports on this site you will find a wealth of international reports as well as reports on specific topics such as female enterprise and high-tech small firms.

The material included in this chapter suggests the following discussion questions:

1. Which of the perspectives reviewed here – glocalization, innovation systems, modes of capitalism and global production chains – provides the most useful framework for understanding the conditions in which entrepreneurs work?
2. What are the strengths and weaknesses of the GEM notion of the Total Entrepreneurial Activity rate? Does this measure provide a robust indication of international contrasts in levels of entrepreneurship? What alternatives would you suggest?
3. What factors might explain the lower level of entrepreneurship activity among women in most countries? How does this relate to notions of 'opportunity' and 'necessity'?

Chapter 3

Enterprising nations

3.1 INTRODUCTION

In the previous chapter we discussed the global landscape of entrepreneurial activity, emphasizing differences between high-income and low-income countries and between opportunity-based and necessity-based entrepreneurship. At the individual level entrepreneurship has the potential to be life sustaining or life changing. For communities, regions and nations, however, entrepreneurship can also have profound implications, increasing their wealth-creating capacity and promoting sustained increases in economic and social development.

In this chapter we focus on these broader – national – consequences of entrepreneurship, emphasizing the role of entrepreneurs in providing new jobs, stimulating innovation and contributing to community stability and cohesion. Strong evidence exists from the US and other more developed economies that entrepreneurship has a role to play in each of these areas. The question is whether these effects of entrepreneurship can always be anticipated; or whether these impacts are conditional on a nation's broader economic and social situation. The answers shed light on the potential for entrepreneurship to contribute to development and social cohesion in each country and also provide an indication of the wider applicability of empirical perspectives derived from analyses conducted in developed economies.

Section 3.2 begins the discussion by outlining the evidence for the impact of entrepreneurship on growth, innovation and cohesion. Section 3.3 then considers the potential for each of these effects in three contrasting countries: Belgium, a high-income European economy; Moldova, an Eastern European transition economy; and Botswana, a middle-income African economy. In each case the nature of entrepreneurial activity differs, as do the broader economic and social conditions. How do these differences influence the impacts of entrepreneurship?

The learning objectives for this chapter are as follows:

■ To introduce students to the main conceptual frameworks linking entrepreneurship to economic growth, technological development and innovation and social cohesion.
■ To allow students to explore the relevance of these conceptual models in alternative international contexts.
■ To encourage a critical perspective on received theory around entrepreneurship and suggest the value of a more contextual approach to the study of entrepreneurial activity.

Further reading and discussion questions are included in Section 3.5.

3.2 ENTREPRENEURSHIP: GROWTH AND DEVELOPMENT EFFECTS

Entrepreneurship and small businesses have been argued to be important for these main reasons. First, in almost all economies around the globe the small business sector is a very significant provider of employment and economic opportunity. Ayyagari *et al.* (2011), for example, compare the contribution to employment of different sizes of firm in a range of different economies around the world (Table 3.1). Whether countries are in the 'high income' or 'low income' groups Ayyagari *et al.*'s analysis suggests that 47–58 per cent of employment is in firms with less than 100 employees, emphasizing the importance of small and medium enterprises (SMEs) as a provider of jobs.

Arguably, however, this contribution to employment underestimates the true, more dynamic, contribution of entrepreneurship and the small firm sector to national economies through their contribution to job creation. This was first

Table 3.1 *Employment contribution of firms of different sizes – by income level of country*

| Firm size band | Income level of country | | | |
| | Low income | Lower-middle income | Upper-middle income | High income |
	% employ.	% employ.	% employ.	% employ.
5–99 employees	57.6	50.9	40.0	46.9
100–249 employees	15.9	15.5	17.5	17.0
250–499 employees	12.0	9.5	11.1	12.7
500 plus employees	13.3	23.3	28.2	24.4

Source: Ayyagari et al. (2011), Figure 5.

highlighted by David Birch (1987) in his influential report *Job Creation in America*. Birch analysed job generation in the USA between 1984 and 1987 and reported that over this period 5 per cent of new ventures had created 87 per cent of the new jobs. His analysis emphasized the importance of small businesses as creators of new jobs and – equally influentially – also introduced a new vocabulary to industrial economics. In particular, Birch suggested that businesses could be divided into three types: elephants – typically large, slow-growth companies that are unresponsive to changes in the economy; mice – small, 'Mom and Pop', no-growth firms that are typically short-lived but reproduce rapidly; and, most interesting, gazelles – new ventures that grow rapidly and are often based on significant technological innovation. Birch's original analysis has been the focus of considerable criticism but his key findings have been verified by a range of other studies in different countries. This has emphasized two 'stylised facts' – findings which appear robust across a wide range of different national contexts (Acs and Mueller, 2008, Henrekson and Johansson, 2010, Parker *et al.*, 2010). First, Birch's overall contention that the small business sector is a key contributor to employment growth has proved robust in a number of different contexts. Ayyagari *et al.* (2011), for example, suggest that between two-thirds and four-fifths of net job creation is attributable to small businesses in a wide range of different economies (Table 3.2). More generally there is evidence from a wide range of different studies using rather different methodologies that in almost all economies net job generation is greatest among small firms. Second, Birch's finding that a very small proportion of start-up companies – 'gazelles' – are responsible for the majority of new job creation has also proved robust in a number of subsequent studies (Henrekson and Johansson, 2010).

Aside from contributing to employment growth, it is argued that entrepreneurship also contributes to economic development by stimulating technological change and innovation, reshaping markets and stimulating economic growth and development (Schumpeter, 1912). In *The Theory of Economic Development* Schumpeter develops a model of technological change as a process of 'creative destruction'. The starting point for this model is to envisage a world (or industry) dominated by smaller firms with rather similar technological capabilities. Knowledge – the basis for innovation – is then assumed to be accessible to each firm in equal measure with some entrepreneurial firms being quicker to 'grab' and implement bits of technology than others. Innovation here generates technology leadership and monopoly power which is at best temporary since it is quickly challenged and eventually eroded by the innovative success of competitors in the following period. Moreover, since the relevant knowledge basis is easily accessible, challenges may come from every quarter. As a consequence, new innovators systematically substitute for incumbents at the frontier of technology. This process is 'creative' in terms of the new innovation and technological progress it generates. It is 'destructive' in terms of the way in which it destroys value in the assets and resources of the firms which are overtaken.

Table 3.2 *Job creation of firms of different sizes – by income level of country*

| Firm size band | Income level of country | | | |
	Low income % employ. growth	Lower-middle income % employ. growth	Upper-middle income % employ. growth	High income % employ. growth
5–99 employees	95.4	71.1	67.5	88.7
100–249 employees	8.6	10.6	11.5	7.9
250–499 employees	3.4	0.4	8.9	4.3
500 plus employees	0.0	0.0	6.8	−4.5

Source: Ayyagari et al. (2011), Figure 7.

Silicon Valley in the USA is often highlighted as the most prominent contemporary example of an entrepreneurial regional innovation system in which creative destruction is evident:

> Silicon Valley has a regional network-based industrial system that promotes collective learning and flexible adjustment amongst specialist producers of a complex of related technologies. The region's dense social networks and open labour markets encourage experimentation and entrepreneurship. Companies compete intensely while at the same time learning from one another about changing markets and technologies through informal communication and collaborative practices; and loosely linked team structures encourage horizontal communication among firm divisions and with outside suppliers and customers. The functional boundaries between firms are porous in a network system, as are the boundaries between firms themselves and between firms and local institutions such as trade associations and universities.
>
> (Saxenian, 1996, pp. 2–3)

What this quote also makes clear, however, is that entrepreneurship in Silicon Valley depends strongly on networks – a development not envisaged in the Schumpeterian model but which reflects recent discussion of open innovation (Elfring and Hulsink, 2003) and the entrepreneurial innovation systems discussed in Chapter 2 (Cooke and Leydesdorff, 2006).

In a situation in which the Schumpeterian process of creative destruction dominates the innovation dynamic within a region or industry we would expect to observe that the typical innovators are small companies, with less innovation

20

among larger firms. But what is the evidence on whether large or small firms dominate innovation? Audretsch (2002), for example, examines US evidence on new product introductions derived from a review of technical journals etc. and examines the small firm share of innovation activity (Table 3.3). In some industries, such as measuring instruments and plastics, he finds that innovation is dominated by smaller firms (Table 3.3); he concludes: 'In some industries such as computers and process control instruments, small firms provide the engine of innovative activity. In other industries, such as pharmaceutical products and aircraft, large firms generate most of the innovative activity' (p. 24).

This suggests that small firms play two rather different roles in innovation. In some industries (measurement, instruments, plastics) it is the small firms themselves which are the innovators. In other sectors – most typically bio-technology – small firms may be the inventors of new technologies but it is larger partner firms which will often undertake the commercialization activity. In this situation the small firm plays the role of inventor, but it is the larger firm which acts as the innovator by bringing the new product or service to market. Audretsch

Table 3.3 Small firms' share of US innovation activity

	Small Firm Share %		Small Firm Share %
Measuring and controlling devices	93.8	Pharmaceutical preparations	37.5
Plastics products	78.8	Plastic materials and resins	33.3
Industrial controls	75.4	Special industry machinery	32.8
Electrical and scientific instruments	65.9	Environmental controls	31.3
Optical instruments and lenses	63.6	Toilet preparations	30.5
Instruments to measure electricity	62.7	Hand and edge tools	28.9
Valves and pipe fittings	62.3	Food products machinery	24.5
Industrial trucks and tractors	60.6	Semiconductors	24.2
Polishes and sanitation goods	59.4	Fabricated plate work	23.7
Electronic computing equipment	59.0	Motors and generators	20.4
Fabricated metal products	58.6	Industrial inorganic chemicals	20.0
Process control instruments	57.8	Surgical appliances and supplies	19.4
Electronic components	57.5	Medicinal and botanicals	15.6
Radio and TV receiving sets	57.1	Office machines	13.0
Surgical and medical instruments	54.5	Electric housewares and fans	11.3
Pumps and pumping equipment	47.1	Photographic equipment	10.2
Radio and TV communications equipment	46.5	Aircraft	3.1

Source: Adapted from Audretsch (2002), Table viii.

(2002) sums this up by concluding that 'the greatest contribution to economic efficiency by small firms is dynamic and evolutionary in nature: Small firms serve as agents of change' (p. 37).

Finally, entrepreneurship and small firms have been argued to be important because of their role in promoting social cohesion and regeneration (Johnson, 2005). Pike *et al.* (2006), for example, comment on European policy and argue that creating new businesses has been seen as a way of stimulating economic activity and helping people make the most of their capabilities. Developing social enterprises such as Mediapila (Box 3.1) may also contribute to economic and social development by bringing marginalized groups into the economic mainstream.

BOX 3.1   MEDIAPILA – AN ARGENTINIAN SOCIAL ENTERPRISE

Mediapila was started in December 2004 when José María Sarasola, who studied Economics and English Literature in Australia, suggested to a group of young people that they needed to do something to improve the impoverished state of Argentina at that time. In March of 2005 José María, together with Joaquín Driollet Laspiur, invested a sum of 14,000 Argentinean pesos ($3,300) and embarked on a project to place industrial sewing machines in the Niño Jesús community soup kitchen in the Chacarita neighborhood of Buenos Aires. In 2005 they worked in the Niño Jesús soup kitchen, where they trained and employed eight women (of these, five now work for Mediapila, one works in an Adidas factory and two have their own shop).

In three months they learned to successfully cut and assemble T-shirts, and set up a professional clothing manufacturing shop. In other words, Mediapila was able to transform the Niño Jesús soup kitchen into a small factory. With the support of Caritas San Isidro, they established another sewing workshop in Pacheco, and with the help of the Fundación Pro Tejer they were able to open Mediapila's first textile training school in the Yayapó soup kitchen, also in Pacheco. Now, Mediapila has its own training centre which provides comprehensive training in the cutting, printing and manufacture of clothing in the Barrio de San Miguel and also has five micro textile mills located in Pacheco, Derqui, San Miguel, Tigre and Chacarita. The key objective of Mediapila remains the textiles training of unemployed women.

Sources: Sarasola and Laspiur (2006) and
http://www.mediapilapais.com/comoempezo.html

Both for-profit entrepreneurship and social enterprise may bring new income streams into an area, improving economic vitality and stability. Such initiatives are often difficult, however, as economically deprived areas tend to lack resources, education and strong local market demands, which can reduce the opportunities for entrepreneurship.

3.3 ENTERPRISING NATIONS COMPARED

The potential value of entrepreneurship and small business as a contributor to job generation, as a source of new innovation and in promoting social cohesion has made entrepreneurship a focal point of policy in the majority of countries. A key question though is whether the stage of development, or the wider economic and social conditions existing in a country may undermine any such efforts. In this section we consider the contrasting role of entrepreneurship in social and economic development in three widely differing countries – Belgium, Moldova and Botswana. Belgium exemplifies the potential role of enterprise as a driver of growth, innovation and cohesion. Moldova in Eastern Europe is an economy in transition in which enterprise is contributing to growth, but due to broader social

---

BOX 3.2 FORMAL AND INFORMAL ENTERPRISE

The informal sector accounts for a significant proportion of economic activity in many developing and transition economies and is often referred to as the 'unregistered', 'unorganized' or 'micro-enterprise' sector. Each of these names gives something of an idea of the nature of the informal sector. In general terms, however, 'informal' enterprises are usually thought of as micro firms operating outside the regulatory and legislative structures which apply to larger firms. A more legal definition was suggested by the International Conference of Labour Statisticians (ICLS) of 1993: Informal enterprises are:

> units engaged in the production of goods and services with the primary objective of generating employment and incomes to the persons involved. These units typically operate at a low level of organisation, with little or no division between labour and capital as factors of production and on a small scale. Labour relations – where they exist – are based mostly on casual employment, kinship or personal and social relations rather than contractual arrangements with formal guarantees.

> Sources: Joshi *et al.* (2011) and Flodman-Becker (2004)

and economic conditions is probably making a weaker contribution to innovation and cohesion. In Botswana, a country bordering South Africa, entrepreneurship may be contributing to growth and cohesion but again its contribution to innovation is perhaps more questionable. Perhaps the key point again is that in each case the social and economic impact of entrepreneurship is highly contextual.

Table 3.4 summarizes the basic economic and demographic data for the three countries. Income per capita is clearly highest in Belgium and lowest in Moldova; Botswana has a middling level of national income although this depends critically on diamond mining. Outside this the Botswana economy is largely rural, dominated by smaller firms and informal enterprise (Box 3.2). GDP growth in both Botswana and Moldova has been substantial in recent years although from a relatively low base in each case. In Botswana HIV/AIDS infection rates are among the highest globally and threaten the otherwise positive pattern of development in the country. For Moldova, a key issue has been out-migration with estimates of the number of migrants ranging from 25 per cent to up to 50 per cent of the economically active population (Pinger, 2010). Even more worrying is that around a third of migrants from Moldova are thought to be highly skilled professionals and university graduates (Pinger, 2010, pp. 145–6). Structural issues in Belgium – as in much of the European Union – relate primarily to low birth rates, increasing life expectancy and an aging population (Table 3.4).

Table 3.4 *Economic and demographic comparisons*

	Belgium	Botswana	Moldova
GDP – per capita	$37,900	$13,100	$2,500
Unemployment rate (%)	8.10	7.50	3.40
Population below poverty line (%)	15.20	30.30	29.50
GDP – real growth rate (%)	1.60	3.10	3.10
Inflation rate (consumer prices) (%)	2.30	7.10	7.30
GDP – composition – agriculture (%)	0.70	2.30	16.30
GDP – composition – industry (%)	22.10	45.80	20.10
GDP – composition – services (%)	77.20	51.90	63.60
Population (m)	10.423	2.029	4.317
Birth rate (births/1,000 population)	10.10	22.54	11.16
Life expectancy at birth – total (years)	79.37	60.93	71.09
HIV/AIDS – adult prevalence rate (%)	0.20	23.90	0.40
Literacy – total (%)	99.00	81.20	99.10
Urbanization – urban population (%)	97	60	42

Source: CIA World Factbook 2011. See: www.theodoria.com.

The three countries also appear very different in terms of the ease of doing business according to the World Bank 'Doing Business' Index. Table 3.5 summarizes the key results for each country giving the country rankings for the overall 'Ease of doing business rank' as well as each of the different dimensions of the ranking. Belgium achieves the highest overall rank of the three countries (25), compared to 52 in Botswana and 90 in Moldova, and the same pattern is repeated over five dimensions of the index: starting a business; dealing with construction permits; protecting investors; trading across borders; and closing a business. Belgium performs less well, however, in terms of registering property and paying taxes.

For Belgium, perhaps as we might have anticipated, there is strong evidence that entrepreneurial activity is contributing to both growth and innovation. The evidence also suggests that these positive effects are strongly reinforcing. De Clercq and Arenius (2006), for example, explore the impact of knowledge-related factors on start-up, comparing Belgium with Finland. This analysis is based on GEM data and focuses on two questions in particular: did respondents 'know someone who had started a business in the last two years' and 'had they personally provided funds for a new business?' Their results for Belgium emphasize the importance of both factors in determining the probability of start-up in Belgium, stressing the value of the availability of external knowledge and examples of success. Manigart and Struyf (1997) also stress the role of finance in early stage start-ups in Belgium, specifically the early stage role of the entrepreneur's own resources and bank lending. Venture capital companies and other private investors

Table 3.5 *Ease of doing business, 2011*

	Belgium	Botswana	Moldova
	Rank out of 183	Rank out of 183	Rank out of 183
Ease of doing business overall rank	25	52	90
Component rankings:			
Starting a business	31	90	94
Dealing with construction permits	41	127	159
Registering property	177	44	18
Getting credit	46	46	89
Protecting investors	16	44	109
Paying taxes	70	21	106
Trading across borders	44	151	141
Enforcing contracts	21	70	20
Closing a business	8	27	92

Source: Doing Business 2011. See: www.doingbusiness.org.

are also important, particularly where larger amounts of risk capital are needed. This again emphasizes the importance of the institutional framework which supports entrepreneurship, particularly where the required investments are substantial and/or a project involves significant risk.

Other studies have suggested that even potentially disadvantaged communities in Belgium achieve each of the benefits of entrepreneurship predicted in earlier sections. Eraydin *et al.* (2010), for example, compare the role of immigrant entrepreneurs in the Belgian city of Antwerp and Izmir in Turkey and emphasize the way in which, given adequate social capital, entrepreneurship generally – and immigrant entrepreneurship more specifically – can contribute to growth, innovation and cohesion. In Antwerp:

> immigrant groups . . . have spread throughout the city, as they have become more entrepreneurial and better integrated. Integration via entrepreneurship thereby seems to have made a positive contribution to the city's general social cohesion, as the amount of interaction between diverse groups has increased. Moreover, Antwerp demonstrates that immigrant entrepreneurship not only contributes to the processes of urban social integration by increasing interaction between groups, but also brings innovations into businesses. Here, from a business point of view, immigrants' innovations can be seen as breaking through existing patterns of production and productivity.
>
> (Eraydin *et al.*, 2010, p. 522)

This positive role of immigrant entrepreneurship in Belgium contrasts sharply with the situation in Moldova, which as we have suggested previously, has suffered from significant out-migration in recent years. As Gorton *et al.* (2004, p. 1252) reported

> in 2002 some 244,000 persons were officially declared as working or looking for work abroad. Unofficial estimates put the level of unemployment and out-migration as much higher, with the latter biased towards the better-educated and younger cohorts of the population.

Pinger (2010) notes the more positive element of this emigration, suggesting that remittances from migrants represent over a fifth of national income in Moldova.

The Moldovan economy was, and remains, largely agricultural with agri-business the dominant industrial sector, although even here industry remains fragmented and productivity remains low (Gorton *et al.*, 2006). Economic development has also been very uneven with a concentration of investment and development in the capital city but a lack of investment and development in more rural – agricultural – areas (Box 3.3: Moldwine). Exports – although significant

– also remain largely agricultural with low levels of value added as firms seek to meet international quality standards (Gorton *et al.*, 2005). Issues also continue to arise in Moldova around some aspects of doing business (Table 3.5) particularly when it comes to public administration and justice, tax administration and international trade, as the cases outlined in Box 3.4 illustrate.

Given the extent of migration from Moldova and the continuing difficulties faced by entrepreneurs within the country, what role is entrepreneurship playing in Moldova's social and economic development? Certainly, small firms remain a very significant source of employment in the country, and entrepreneurship – whether illegal, informal or legal – represents a potentially important driver of economic growth. The role of entrepreneurial activity in promoting either innovation or social cohesion seems less evident given the extent and nature of migration from the country.

Finally, in Botswana the economy is strongly diamond-dependent and the government is seeking to diversify the economy by strengthening the small business sector. Small, medium and micro enterprise (SMME) development is seen as a priority but the sector remains dominated by the very large informal sector: the 'informal sector is the portion of a country's economy that is outside the regulatory environment and whose activities are hardly reflected in official statistics' (Mutula and Van Brakel, 2007, p. 231). More generally, however, most firms remain small, focused on local markets and strongly restricted by shortages of finance (Ngowi *et al.*, 2002) and higher-level skills (Mutula and Van Brakel, 2007). Ngowi *et al.* (2002), for example, studied the ability of ten 'citizen-owned' construction companies in Botswana to access finance and concluded that firms found it difficult to access finance and had to adopt other competitive strategies to generate growth.

BOX 3.3 MOLDWINE

Moldwine was originally established in the 1950s as a grape collecting and processing centre. When the company was privatized in 1999 it employed 33 staff. The firm's pre-privatization director bought up many of the shares in the company and built up a controlling ownership stake. Key issues highlighted by researchers working with the company were the poor technological base within the plant, the lack of any well-developed marketing or promotional plan and a lack of any clear strategy for procurement or development. Researchers from Liverpool University in the UK began working with the company on an action research case study focused on trying to help the company to develop its capabilities in procurement, technology and marketing.

Source: Gorton *et al.* (2005)

BOX 3.4   SHADES OF ENTREPRENEURSHIP IN MOLDOVA

Welter and Smallbone (2011) provide two illustrations of the difficulties faced by entrepreneurs in Moldova and their engagement with the administration of justice and the black (criminal) and grey (informal) economies. They highlight the case of one female entrepreneur:

It took her several months to register her business and obtain licenses. For each document she brought, clerks asked for payment or presents, sometimes having established fixed sums per document. Once up and running, she needed to continue bribing the police . . . the day before the interview, her driver had been stopped four times, each time paying a 'fine' to four different officials from the State Traffic Inspectorate (p. 110).

Welter and Smallbone (2011) also report a second case of an entrepreneur operating a legally registered private limited company:

despite this . . . parts of its activities are still illegal. For example, when crossing the border, the entrepreneur usually declares lower quantities in his documents and lower costs for his goods in order to avoid customs dues. Several studies have shown the frequent occurrence of such avoidance behaviours of entrepreneurs in early stages of transition.

Source: Welter and Smallbone (2011)

To explore the availability of higher-level skills in Botswana, Mutula and Van Brakel (2007) used focus group and company interviews to examine ICT expertise; this study highlighted generally low levels of ICT skills. Hence they argue that: 'If ICT skills challenges are not addressed urgently, Botswana could lose its economic advantages in the connected world because of the migrating IT specialists, a small IT workforce or the low ratio of ICT graduates' (p. 243).

Unlike the situation in Belgium, studies of entrepreneurship in Botswana also tend to highlight the difficulties faced by women and minority groups in entrepreneurship rather than the positive contribution of such groups to cohesion. Hanson (2009), for example, summarizes the results from research by Hovorka (2006) in Gaborone, which focused on 109 urban, commercial and agricultural enterprises, roughly half of which were owned by women. She notes that:

Compared to men's enterprises, women's are more likely to be located on the home plot of land, on smaller plots, and on land that is less desirable for farming; they are also more likely to be smaller in scale, to be less capital intensive, to employ fewer people, and to yield lower incomes.

(Hanson, 2009, p. 255)

The motives for entrepreneurial activity in Botswana may also be different to that elsewhere. Focusing on women entrepreneurs, Hanson (2009) notes a wide variety of motivations 'from survival to increased income and status. The context of rapid urbanization and agrarian change in Botswana has provided openings for women to transform their lives' (p. 256). Other studies have suggested a lack of entrepreneurial aspiration among some groups of the population in Botswana. Plattner *et al.* (2009), for example, report a relatively low level of self-belief and entrepreneurial aspiration among undergraduate students. Of 329 respondents only 8 reported that they wanted to be entrepreneurs, although in some cases necessity may force graduates to rethink this position (Box 3.5).

The locally focused nature of much entrepreneurial activity in Botswana – both formal and informal – may ensure that entrepreneurship and small business are

---

BOX 3.5 CLEANING-UP IN BOTSWANA

In 2005 Kgosietsile Mariri graduated from the University of Botswana after majoring in Sociology. After spending a long time searching for employment without success, Mariri decided to venture into self-employment by buying the 'Pula Dry Cleaners' in Maruapula. According to Mariri, when he bought the business it was in such a terrible state that the Citizen Entrepreneurship Development Agency (CEDA) was uncomfortable about financing it – the machinery and the building were too old to cope with the day-to-day running of the business or to attract customers.

Narrating his story Mariri said: 'I want to modernise the industry to make it fashionable in terms of everything . . . I had a plan of what I wanted to do in this business sector dominated by older people.' Renaming the company (C'est Magnifique Dry Cleaners), improving the marketing and advertising of the company and finally getting support from CEDA to purchase new capital equipment, Mariri now employs six full-time workers. Mariri advised other young people who want to venture into business to go to CEDA 'as it is open to every person in Botswana'. He said they should be patient with making profit as it usually takes time for a business to yield the expected returns.

Source: Article by Tumelo Setshogo, 'A focused entrepreneur',
published online on 15th August 2008 and available at
http://www.mmegi.bw

contributing to local cohesion (McDade and Spring, 2005). There is also clear evidence that entrepreneurial activity is contributing to growth by providing new jobs and opportunities for both male and female entrepreneurs. It is more difficult perhaps to sustain an argument that entrepreneurial activity is contributing strongly to innovation in Botswana given the difficulties firms face in accessing financial resources and higher-level skills.

Perhaps the key point to emerge from the comparison of these three countries is the challenge their examples pose to any assumption that entrepreneurship will always contribute to growth, innovation and cohesion. Instead, the impact of entrepreneurship on each aspect of economic and social development is seen to be strongly contextual. In Belgium, high levels of social and institutional capital were enhancing – or perhaps enabling – the growth potential of entrepreneurship, an effect which was weaker or absent in Moldova and Botswana. Similarly, high levels of knowledge availability and higher-level skills in Belgium were enhancing, or again perhaps enabling, entrepreneurship to contribute to innovation, impacts which were again more limited in Moldova and Botswana. In Moldova too, local entrepreneurial activity was also clearly insufficient to outweigh the perceived benefits of international migration opportunities. Here, entrepreneurship may have been contributing to cohesion, but in isolation it was clearly unable to ensure demographic stability. In short, while entrepreneurship certainly has the potential to contribute to growth, innovation and cohesion, these effects cannot be taken for granted.

3.4 SUMMARY AND KEY POINTS

There is substantial evidence that entrepreneurship can make a positive contribution to business and economic growth, innovation and social cohesion. Evidence on the importance of each effect, however, comes largely from more developed economies, with a much weaker evidence base in transition and developing economies. The ability of entrepreneurship to contribute to growth is, for example, strongly conditional on the availability of finance and an appropriate skill base; without either the potential growth of enterprises may be substantially constrained. Finance and skill availability are also crucial if entrepreneurship is to contribute to innovation although here other factors such as a local market for relatively sophisticated products/services may also be important.

In policy terms the contextual nature of the impact of entrepreneurship on growth, innovation and social cohesion suggests the limitations of entrepreneurship or SME policy where it is considered in isolation from other aspects of policy development. This is also one of the key messages of the World Bank's 'Doing Business' project, which stresses both the positive developmental effects of entrepreneurship and the importance of the wider business environment. In more conceptual terms the differential impacts of entrepreneurship in Botswana,

Belgium and Moldova emphasize the value of an institutional or neo-institutional perspective on entrepreneurship which locates entrepreneurship within a specific institutional context. Where the institutional context is appropriate, growth, innovation and social cohesion effects may result; where institutions are weak or disabling, such effects are less likely. Whatever the institutional context, however, individuals, and individual decisions, are at the heart of the entrepreneurial process. The next two chapters focus on the characteristics and behaviours of individual entrepreneurs and the factors which come together to shape the decision to become an entrepreneur.

3.5 DISCUSSION QUESTIONS AND FURTHER READING

A wealth of additional material is available which profiles the impact of entrepreneurship on the social and economic development of individual countries. For more data on the impact of small firms on employment growth in different countries see the tables in Ayyagari *et al.* (2011). GEM reports on different countries also contain an expert commentary and these often highlight the country-specific barriers to entrepreneurship (http://www.gemconsortium.org). Welter and Smallbone (2011) provide a very accessible account of the issues faced by entrepreneurs in a range of difficult environments. See Eraydin *et al.* (2010) for the counter case. More generally see Parker *et al.* (2010) for a good review on the evidence on job creation and Henrekson and Johansson (2010) for an excellent article on the role of gazelle companies in stimulating growth.

The issues covered in this chapter suggest the following questions for discussion:

1   Which of the three development effects of entrepreneurship – job creation, innovation or cohesion – is most important? Does this differ between developed and developing economies?

2   What do the contrasting effects of entrepreneurship in Moldova, Belgium and Botswana suggest about the nature of entrepreneurial activity?

3   What are the key difficulties facing entrepreneurs in Moldova? What steps could the government take to reduce these barriers?

4   How would you describe the entrepreneurial decision made by Kgosietsile Mariri (Box 3.5)? What could have been done to support his business?

Chapter 4

Who are the entrepreneurs?

4.1 INTRODUCTION

In previous chapters we have outlined institutional theories of enterprise which suggest that the business and economic environment in which entrepreneurs operate will shape their activities and will, in part at least, determine levels of entrepreneurial activity (Bruton *et al.*, 2009). In European and some Asian economies, for example, the stigma attached to business failure has often been said to be a greater barrier to entrepreneurship than it is in the USA. In 2010, for example, 26.7 per cent of adults in the USA said fear of failure would prevent them starting a business compared to 40.5 per cent in France and 50.9 per cent in Greece (GEM, 2010, pp. 17–18). These differences may help to explain part or all of the difference in entrepreneurship rates in the US and Europe and also between regions within individual countries. Vaillant and Lafuente (2007), for example, argue that the potential stigma of business failure is a significant determinant of differences in entrepreneurial activity between different parts of rural Spain. In other emerging economies lack of finance, or the difficulty of enforcing property rights, have also been said to have a significant effect on the level of entrepreneurial activity (Stenning *et al.*, 2010).

In terms of institutional theory both of these aspects of the business environment – the stigma of failure, lack of finance – are regarded as elements of 'structure', i.e. the set of economic and social conditions within which individuals or firms make strategic choices. As Bruton *et al.* suggest: 'The institutional perspective directs attention to the rules, norms and beliefs that influence organizations and their members, which can vary widely across countries and within cultures' (Bruton *et al.*, 2010, p. 421). But structure alone cannot explain why a specific individual or firm makes an entrepreneurial decision or begins a new start-up company. In terms of institutional theory these individual – entrepreneurial – responses to structure are called 'agency'. But what determines an individual's decision to become an entrepreneur? Or, in the terms of institutional theory, what shapes the individual agent's response to structure? This is the focus of this chapter, which explores in more detail the personal characteristics and motivations of individual entrepreneurs.

Some of the personal characteristics of entrepreneurs are easily visible, of course. Bio-demographic characteristics such as gender, ethnicity and age are readily observable and numerous previous studies have suggested that such characteristics play an important part in shaping entrepreneurial activity. Gender, for example, is shown by Karupiah (2010) to be a significant determinant of entrepreneurial choice by graduates in Malaysia (Aidis *et al.*, 2007). Ethnicity and religion can also play an important part in shaping, and enabling, the development of agency (Essers and Benschop, 2009). Similarly, Kautonen *et al.* (2010) argue that age – which they argue is strongly linked to work experience – may also shape an individual's entrepreneurial intentions. Other personal characteristics such as education, experience, location and family background are also relatively easy to identify and have often been linked to entrepreneurship (Carter and Marlow, 2007). Other potentially important factors such as optimism, self-belief or ambition, however, are much more difficult to measure making research more difficult as we shall see (Storey, 2011).

The rest of the chapter is organized as follows. Section 4.2 focuses on the role and interaction of structure and agency in shaping the entrepreneurial decision. Subsequent sections focus on the empirical evidence dealing first with bio-demographic, behavioural and cognitive influences on entrepreneurship. Section 4.5 then outlines some evidence from integrating studies which reflect both structural and agentic influences on the entrepreneurship decision.

The main learning objectives for this chapter are as follows:

- To introduce students to the key aspects of institutional theory in the context of the entrepreneurial decision. To introduce the concepts of structure and agency.
- To consider the evidence on the bio-demographic, behavioural and cognitive influences on entrepreneurial behaviour and the relevance of these in alternative international contexts.
- To provide students with an understanding of the potential interactions of structural and agentic influences on entrepreneurial behaviour.

Further reading and discussion questions are included in Section 4.7.

4.2 STRUCTURE, AGENCY AND THE ENTREPRENEURSHIP DECISION

A recent study by Lu and Tao (2010) investigates the role of institutional and personal characteristics on the entrepreneurship decision in China; this study provides a useful example of the way in which institutional and personal characteristics interact to shape the entrepreneurship decision. More specifically, Lu and Tao (2010) suggest a theoretical framework in which the impact of personal characteristics on the entrepreneurship decision is moderated by the institutional structure (Figure 4.1).

In their empirical analysis of the entrepreneurship decision Lu and Tao (2010) find considerable support for the influence of individual attributes and the institutional environment. There is also clear evidence of the hypothesized moderating effect of the institutional environment on the effect of individual attributes; for example, a key variable in their representation of the institutional environment in China is the legal status of private sector enterprises which changed significantly in 1989. Lu and Tao's analysis suggests that this change moderates the effects of a range of personal characteristics (age, marital status, education) on the entrepreneurship decision. Prior to the change in legal structure personal characteristics were more important in shaping the entrepreneurial decision than post-1989. As Lu and Tao (2010) conclude, 'we find strong support for the role of institutional environment for the entrepreneurship decision, and for the personal attributes of would be entrepreneurs' (p. 272).

Other studies have highlighted the differences in the institutional context for entrepreneurship between developed and emerging economies and the implications for the entrepreneurship decision (Puffer et al., 2010). In general, such studies have suggested the negative effect of the weaker institutional support for entrepreneurship in emerging and transition economies, and have argued that this is likely to be a barrier to entrepreneurial activity. As discussed in Chapter 2, however, this is not always what we observe, with levels of entrepreneurial activity often higher in developing and transition economies. A nation's institutional environment may also stimulate different types of entrepreneurial activity, building on individual attributes. McDade and Spring (2005), for example, highlight what they call a 'new generation' of African entrepreneurs who are building on their international work and networking experience. Importantly too, McDade and Spring (2005) emphasize the role of these entrepreneurs in reshaping the institutional

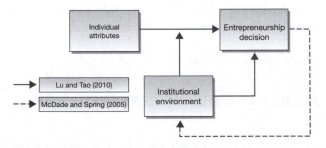

Figure 4.1
What determines the entrepreneurial decision?
Source: Adapted from Lu and Tao (2010) and McDade and Spring (2005).

environment for entrepreneurial activity. The potential for this 'institutional work' (McDade and Spring, 2005) suggests an extension of the framework outlined by Lu and Tao (2010) to include potentially positive feedbacks from individual entrepreneurship decisions to the institutional environment (Figure 4.1).

4.3 BIO-DEMOGRAPHIC CHARACTERISTICS

Bio-demographic factors such as age, gender, ethnicity and marital status are often included in studies of entrepreneurship as control factors intended to isolate the effects of other – perhaps more interesting – issues. However, the effects of these variables are often substantial with levels of entrepreneurial activity varying widely by age group and gender. Some commonalities are also evident, however, between the bio-demographic characteristics of entrepreneurs in different countries. GEM data suggests, for example, that entrepreneurship activity tends to be highest in the 25–34 and 35–44 age groups across all groups of countries (Table 4.1). Likewise, female engagement with enterprise is more limited than that of males in most countries as the discussion in Chapter 2 suggests.

A recent survey-based study of women entrepreneurs in the Middle East and North Africa (MENA) countries emphasizes a similar point, suggesting analogous profiles of the age distribution and marital status of women entrepreneurs across a range of different countries (CAWTAR/IFC, 2007). More variation is evident, however, in the educational level of the women entrepreneurs in each country (Table 4.2). In Bahrain, for example, 60.8 per cent of women entrepreneurs had a university degree compared to only 19.4 per cent of those surveyed in Lebanon. To some extent, as suggested by the model proposed earlier by Lu and Tao (2010), this reflects the culture of the different MENA countries and the extent of educational opportunities available to women in each country. Case studies from

Table 4.1 *TEA rates for women early stage entrepreneurs, 2007*

	Europe and Asian middle-income countries	*Latin American and Caribbean middle-income countries*	*High-income countries*
	% Population	*% Population*	*% Population*
Age group			
18–24 years	8.7	11.7	2.5
25–34 years	10.0	17.2	6.4
35–44 years	8.8	17.8	5.5
45–54 years	6.2	14.6	4.1
55–64 years	2.8	6.8	2.3

Source: GEM 2007 Report on Women and Entrepreneurship, Figure 4, p. 28.

35

Table 4.2 *Characteristics of women entrepreneurs in the MENA countries*

	Bahrain N = 99	Jordan N = 96	Lebanon N = 95	Tunisia N = 97	UAE N = 96
Age distribution					
Under 25	0.0	6.1	1.0	2.1	0.0
25–34	18.2	39.8	30.3	30.9	26.3
35–44	46.5	35.7	29.3	32.0	43.2
45–54	32.3	14.3	26.3	29.9	26.3
55 or older	3.0	4.1	13.1	5.2	4.2
Marital status					
Married	65.7	63.5	58.9	74.2	67.7
Single	12.1	20.8	22.1	18.6	14.6
Divorced	12.1	3.1	8.4	4.1	13.5
Separated	10.1	6.3	1.1	0.0	3.1
Widowed	0.0	6.3	9.5	3.1	0.0
Education					
Primary	0.0	3.0	17.2	4.1	8.6
Secondary	6.2	20.2	39.8	15.3	6.5
Some post-secondary	25.8	24.2	22.6	10.2	11.8
University degree	60.8	43.4	19.4	57.1	38.7
Postgraduate	7.2	9.1	1.1	13.3	34.4

Source: CAWTAR/IFC (2007), pp. 60–78.

the same report, however, emphasize the success of women entrepreneurs in the MENA countries (Box 4.1).

Which of these demographic factors are most important in determining whether people become entrepreneurs? Taniguchi (2002) provides some evidence for women's self-employment in the USA examining both a number of observable demographic and more socially determined factors. In Table 4.3 we summarize the results of this multivariate analysis where we use '+' or '−' to indicate statistically significant or robust positive or negative effects and symbols in brackets to indicate less statistically robust effects. Four factors increase the probability of becoming self-employed: prior work or self-employment experience, experience of a professional occupation, being married and having older children. Age, and being a member of the African-American community, reduces the probability of being self-employed, while other factors – including education – prove less significant.

BOX 4.1   ENTREPRENEURIAL AGENCY: WOMEN ENTREPRENEURS IN THE MIDDLE EAST

Huda Janahi, Bahrain, global freight and passenger services

Huda Janahi was a housewife. She graduated from an entrepreneurship training programme – the Bahrain Model of Investment Promotion & Enterprise Creation – and developed a business idea for transport and cargo services. In the first instance, the business registration authorities rejected the idea by claiming, 'This business is not for women'. Despite the odds, Huda Janahi started her business 'Global Cargo' in 2001 with a small office, a staff of two people and an initial investment of $4,000.

By 2010 the company was managing business assets worth around $3 million and was one of the leading cargo and travel services in Bahrain, with 28 staff. Huda Janahi commented:

> I think one of the most important factors in my success is in my reliance on experts' opinion provided to me by bank directors, economists and senior experts, which I consider a fundamental principle for the success of any project . . . In addition to this, I count on the values of integrity and honesty stemming from our religion, and strongly believe in consulting, quality, flexibility and teamwork.

Huda Janahi has received numerous recognitions and awards from various institutions, business forums and magazines including being ranked 46th by *Forbes* magazine in their list of the 50 most powerful Arab businesswomen.

Hazar Mirabi Salam, Lebanon, engineering services

Hazar Mirabi Salam is a Lebanese businesswoman in her mid-fifties who runs a private company providing engineering services in Lebanon and internationally. The first project she designed and carried out was in Tripoli, where she designed the premises of Middle East Airlines. Afterwards, she designed four restaurants in Beirut Airport. After succeeding in submitting the best offer for the design, she was denied the work because the general director at that time did not want a woman to carry out the project. Hazar Salam emphasizes the importance of entrepreneurship for women: 'if there is no work available for them, to invent it as a gateway to social, emotional and economic safety and a means to build up the personality and highlight their potential'.

Hazar's design talents were discovered at school. She ended up obtaining an engineering degree. She entered the world of business as soon as she graduated and worked with some of her professors.

As I highly value freedom and autonomy, I decided to open my own office. I was 27 when I created my own office with some of my colleagues. At the beginning I started to work alone, assisted by only one person in the workshop.

Later she combined family life and work:

My stability at home helped me to enhance my devotion and commitment to work; so I went on working from home with the assistance of women engineers who helped me design maps and carry them out. . . . I always preferred working with young women because they are more committed and accurate in addition to being more resolute to remain in Lebanon; this is as opposed to young men who, most of them, have this temptation to emigrate.

Sources: CAWTAR/IFC (2007) and
http://www.arceit.org/content/success-stories.html

These results are not perhaps very surprising but it is difficult to know whether the specific factors highlighted by Taniguchi (2002) for the USA are reflected elsewhere. Differences in cultural factors – elements of structure – are clearly important and as the model proposed by Lu and Tao (2010) suggests individual attributes might interact with elements of the institutional environment to shape the entrepreneurship decision. In short, bio-demographic factors and other individual characteristics are clearly important but an individual's decision to become an entrepreneur remains strongly contingent on the institutional context.

4.4 BEHAVIOURAL AND COGNITIVE PERSPECTIVES

In entrepreneurship research alongside bio-demographic factors there is a long tradition of trying to identify personality traits which make entrepreneurs different from other members of the population. Knight (1921), for example, argued that entrepreneurs are more willing to bear risk than others. For McClelland (1961) entrepreneurship was more strongly linked to certain personality types which are more highly motivated to seek achievement. A slightly different take on the same drive for achievement emphasizes what is called 'locus of control' (Rotter, 1966), and the entrepreneur's belief that the success of a venture or an enterprise 'all depends on me'. Others have seen entrepreneurship as a reaction to low self-esteem or negative formative experiences which may lead individuals to

Table 4.3 *Determinants of entry into self-employment: women, USA*

Factor	Effect	Factor	Effect
Occupation		Personal/work characteristics	
Professional	+	Part-time	(−)
Managerial	(+)	Education (years)	(+)
Sales	(+)	Married	+
Crafts, operatives and farmers	(+)	No. of younger children	(−)
Labourers	(+)	No. of older children	+
Service	+	Previously self-employed	+
Private household workers	+	Age	−
		Number of previous jobs	+
Race and ethnicity		Prior work experience	+
African-American	−		
Hispanic	(−)		

Note: '+' denotes a positive and significant effect; '−' denotes a negative and significant effect.
Source: Taniguch: (2002), Table 1, p. 884.

adopt abnormal, or in psychological terms 'deviant', behaviours in order to succeed (De Vries, 1977). Other writers – perhaps based more on impression than evidence – have argued that these traits are not important. Drucker (1993), for example, argues that:

> Entrepreneurship is . . . not a personality trait; in thirty years I have seen people of the most diverse personalities and temperaments perform well in entrepreneurial challenges. To be sure, people who need certainty are unlikely to make good entrepreneurs. But such people are unlikely to do well in a host of other activities as well.

Similarly, Aldrich (1999) comments: 'Research on personal traits seems to have reached an empirical dead end' (p. 76).

More recently, however, there has been something of a renewed interest in the entrepreneurial personality. Rauch and Frese (2007), for example, conduct a meta-study reviewing a wide range of papers which have examined the relationship between entrepreneur and business owner personality traits and performance. They start by highlighting the very wide range of around fifty personality characteristics which have been linked to entrepreneurial behaviour (Table 4.4).

Based on an analysis of the results of previous studies Rauch and Frese (2007, p. 369) find

> that business owners' personality traits were positively related to business creation and business success . . . [and] additional traits that are important

Table 4.4 *Entrepreneurial characteristics linked to performance*

Aggressiveness	Goal orientation	Proactive personality
Benevolence	Higher order need strength	Protestant work ethic beliefs
Conformity	Humility	Rigidity
Conscientiousness	Impulsiveness	Risk-taking propensity
Conservatism	Innovativeness	Scepticism
Creativity	Internal locus of control	Self-confidence
Delay of gratification	Need for achievement	Self-efficacy
Discipline	Need for affiliation	Self-esteem
Dogmatism	Need for autonomy	Self-reliance
Emotional stability	Need for dominance	Shyness
Endurance	Neuroticism	Sobriety
Enthusiasm	Norm orientation	Stress tolerance
Expedience	Openness to experience	Tenacity
Extraversion	Optimism	Tolerance for ambiguitya
Flexibility	Originality	Tough-mindedness
Forthrightness	Passion for work	Trustworthy
Future orientation	Practicality	

Source: Rauch and Frese (2007), Table 1.

predictors of entrepreneurial behaviour: innovativeness, proactive personality, generalized self-efficacy, stress tolerance, need for autonomy, and internal locus of control were related to entrepreneurial behaviour.

This, they suggest, means that entrepreneurship research needs to take personality seriously in assessing the factors which both determine business start-up and business success. Rauch and Frese (2007, p. 372) also note, however, that it is important that such analyses are grounded firmly in their specific context:

Personality traits can affect behaviour only if situations are relevant and not constrained to allow the expression of individual differences. Thus, potential moderators are environmental constraints such as the economic situation at the time of study, the demands of the specific industry, or the stage in the business life cycle. Unfavourable environments may constrain the expression of individual differences. Favourable environments may allow the expression of individual traits, for example, owners with a high need for achievement may be able to pursue more opportunities than owners with a low need for achievement.

Reflecting the arguments made in neo-institutional theories, this again suggests the need for a contingent approach in which both the characteristics (personality traits) and the situation of the entrepreneur are considered together (Lu and Tao, 2010).

4.5 PUTTING IT ALL TOGETHER

Two relatively new and integrative types of research studies have emerged which have tried to integrate the type of entrepreneurial characteristics (or agent level) factors discussed in the previous sections with broader social and economic indicators, i.e. structure. In each type of study the central question is whether the entrepreneurship decision is primarily one of structure or agency. The first group of studies is based on comparative surveys of entrepreneurs and non-entrepreneurs. One such study, by Djankov *et al.* (2006), compared entrepreneurs and non-entrepreneurs in China and Russia where entrepreneurs are defined as owner-managers of businesses with five or more employees and non-entrepreneurs as individuals who do not own a business (Box 4.2). Survey data was collected on a random sample from around 400 entrepreneurs in each country and a similarly sized group of non-entrepreneurs matched by age, gender and educational attainment. Because Djankov *et al.* (2006) were basing their analysis on survey data they were able to get rich attitudinal and situational data about their respondents reflecting both elements of structure and individual agency.

Djankov *et al.* (2006) focus on what factors influence the probability that an individual will become an entrepreneur rather than a non-entrepreneur, using a series of multivariate probit models to explore how different factors explain the probability of being an entrepreneur. Table 4.5 includes their models for Russia and China with statistically robust coefficients indicated by stars. In the table the coefficients can be interpreted as the change in the probability of becoming an entrepreneur if an individual has a particular characteristic. For example, in Russia, individuals whose father was a member of the Communist party were 10.8 per cent more likely to become an entrepreneur. So what are the key findings? First, Communist party links tend to matter in Russia but not in China. Second, in both countries having family or friends who are entrepreneurs increases the probability that an individual will become an entrepreneur. Third, Djankov *et al.* find mixed evidence on the importance of cognitive capabilities and attitudes to risk but do find that 'greed' is positively associated with the probability of becoming an entrepreneur in both countries. (Greed is measured by whether individuals are likely to retire if they win a large amount of money on a lottery or whether they would continue to work as they want more money.) Rather more strangely, individuals' height also matters with shorter people more likely to be entrepreneurs in Russia, while in China taller people were more likely to be entrepreneurs. Djankov *et al.* offer no explanation for this latter result.

The Djankov *et al.* study suggests that elements of structure (e.g. family background, entrepreneurial friends) and agency (e.g. greed, attitudes to risk)

41

BOX 4.2 ENTREPRENEURIAL AGENCY IN CHINA AND RUSSIA – FENG JUN AND YULIA BARABASHEVA

Feng Jun is CEO of Aigo, one of China's fastest growing electronics firms. Feng studied civil engineering at Beijing's Tsinghua University. He then got a master's degree in business administration from Peking University. He went on to work for a government construction company before he quit to start Aigo, known in Mandarin as Aiguozhe or 'Patriot', which started selling keyboards to China's infant computer industry.

Aigo took off in the mid-1990s when it started making portable computer memory devices. Aigo has subsequently expanded its range of products sold in its orange-and-white packaging to include digital cameras, MP3 devices, portable media players and a digital microscope. Its 1,700-strong workforce includes 700 people in product development. Revenue is growing by 60 to 70 per cent a year, with 80 per cent of profits ploughed back into research.

As of 2011 Feng Jun remains the President and sole shareholder of Aigo. He is Chairman of the Tshinghua Entrepreneur & Executive Club as well as being a member of the China Entrepreneur Club (CEC). He has won a range of awards including being named as a Davos World Economic Forum Young Global Leader in 2007.

Yulia Barabasheva (25) is a reluctant entrepreneur. She never wanted to have her own beauty salon, but with a dream of securing a steadier income and starting a family she opened her beauty salon in Moscow in April 2007. Now, she and her staff of 14 take clients up to 12 hours a day, seven days a week, giving them thinner eyebrows or exciting nails. Yulia's husband, Igor Barabashev, a businessman, was able to get $180,000 in start-up loans and complete a six-month trail through Russia's formidable business bureaucracy to obtain a licence for Yulia's business.

Born to teenage parents on the outskirts of Moscow and in her own apartment by the age of 16, Yulia passed high school by showing up just for exams and worked in construction and a liquor factory before turning to nail design. After some years working for other people in another beauty salon she finally left to found her own studio.

Sources: *Marketing News*, 1 September 2008 and biography at http://www.dld-conference.com/speakers/digital-business/feng-jun_aid_727.html (accessed 3 September 2011); *The Christian Science Monitor*, 27 February 2008

Table 4.5 Probit models of being an entrepreneur: China and Russia

Explanatory variables	Russia Coeff.	SE.	China Coeff.	SE.
Father with secondary or higher education	−0.014	0.012	0.004	0.007
Father member of Communist party	0.108*	0.023	0.011	0.023
Mother was boss or director	0.371*	0.136	0.066	0.047
Mother with secondary or higher education	−0.013	0.009	−0.016*	0.008
Family members entrepreneurs	0.050*	0.003	0.012*	0.007
Friends who are entrepreneurs	0.075*	0.009	0.032*	0.011
Cognitive test score	−0.006	0.007	0.003	0.005
Height	−0.005*	0.001	0.001*	0.000
Risk loving	−0.033*	0.009	0.080*	0.006
Top 10 per cent in school (self-reported)	0.087*	0.011	−0.009	0.010
Greed	0.097*	0.019	0.155*	0.015
City favourable to entrepreneurs	0.035**	0.17	0.011	0.011
Govt. favourable to entrepreneurs	0.006	0.006	−0.001	0.006
Observations	726		804	

Source: Njankov et al. (2006), Table 2.

work together to influence the probability that any specific individual will become an entrepreneur. This reflects the findings of Lu and Tao (2010) discussed earlier and also the suggestion from Rauch and Frese (2007) that both structure and agency need to be considered as part of the entrepreneurial decision. The Djankov *et al.* study also suggests, however, that the balance of influence between structure and agency may differ between countries. Elements of structure – locational factors, for example – seem to matter more in Russia than in China.

The second group of studies which offer new insights into the determinants of entrepreneurship relate to genetic predispositions towards enterprise (Johnson, 2009, Nicolaou and Shane, 2010, Nicolaou *et al.*, 2008, 2009, Zhang *et al.*, 2009). The series of studies by Nicolaou and his co-authors is particularly insightful, combining a range of genetic and societal factors. Key to these studies is the use of data on pairs of identical (monozygotic) and non-identical (dizygotic) twins. As identical twins share all of their genes and non-identical twins 50 per cent of their genes on average, differences in behaviour between pairs of twins within the groups can be attributed to the genetic differences. Nicolaou *et al.* (2008) highlight four mechanisms through which individuals' genetic make-up might influence entrepreneurship behaviour. First, they argue that individuals' genetic make-up might influence brain chemistry to make individuals more or less risk averse or tolerant of uncertainty. This, in turn, may influence individual willingness to

43

become an entrepreneur. Second, genetic make-up may predispose the development of personality traits associated with entrepreneurship – extraversion, for example (Table 4.4). Third, they argue that genetic make-up may encourage individuals to select into environments which are more conducive to entrepreneurship such as higher education. Finally, genetic make-up may influence some individuals to be more responsive to stimuli which prompt entrepreneurial activity. Nicolaou *et al.* (2008) use data from a large sample of UK female twins to explore the hypothesis that genetic factors are associated with entrepreneurship and, using a range of different indicators of entrepreneurial activity, conclude that between 37 and 42 per cent of the variability in the probability of being an entrepreneur can be linked to genetic factors. The other 58–63 per cent of the variation in the probability of being an entrepreneur is determined by environmental factors. They conclude:

> . . . our results indicate that genetic factors influence the tendency to become an entrepreneur. However, they do not indicate that entrepreneurship is genetically predetermined . . . environmental factors . . . explain much of the variance in entrepreneurial activity, providing strong evidence of the effect of environmental factors on the propensity to become an entrepreneur.
>
> (Nicolaou *et al.* 2008, p. 174)

Subsequent studies have largely confirmed these initial results using samples of male twins from the USA with almost identical results (Nicolaou and Shane, 2010).

4.6 SUMMARY AND KEY POINTS

Recent evidence sheds much light on the characteristics of typical entrepreneurs – if indeed there can be said to be such a person – and the determinants of entrepreneurship activity. In terms of institutional theory, elements of both structure and agency seem important with the impact of individual characteristics strongly contingent on elements of the business environment. Similarly, genetic research suggests that while a significant proportion of the variation in entrepreneurship can be explained in terms of individuals' genetic make-up, environmental influences – or structure – remain important. Developments in genetic research do, however, suggest a need for the re-evaluation of the standard notion of 'agency' in determining entrepreneurship. In particular, it suggests the limits of 'agency' with agents' degree of free will or self-determination shaped by their genetic legacy. This suggests some potentially fascinating lines of new research. How, for example, does individual predisposition towards entrepreneurship – stemming from genetic make-up – differ between cultures and nationalities?

What effect does this have on levels of entrepreneurial activity given differences in operating environments?

Finally, it is worth recalling why it actually matters whether it is genetics, traits or experience which determine levels of entrepreneurial activity. If entrepreneurship is purely genetic, for example, issues of nurture, experience and training would matter little and we might expect levels of entrepreneurial activity to be broadly similar across countries. But, as previous chapters have emphasized, this is not what we observe. Instead, levels of entrepreneurial activity vary widely, reflecting national economic and social conditions. In other words, structure matters greatly both in terms of its direct influence on levels of entrepreneurial activity and in terms of its interaction with individual predisposition towards entrepreneurship. Public policy remains important therefore, both in shaping the environment for entrepreneurship and in influencing individuals' entrepreneurship decisions.

4.7 DISCUSSION QUESTIONS AND FURTHER READING

Central to the argument in this chapter are the role of structure and agency in whether an individual choses to become an entrepreneur. On the interaction of structure and agency in China see Lu and Tao (2010), on Africa see McDade and Spring (2005) and on Belgium see Eraydin *et al.* (2010). More recent studies focusing on genetic explanations for entrepreneurship pose challenges to the notion of 'agency' itself. On this see Nicolaou and Shane (2010).

The arguments in this chapter suggest the following questions for discussion:

1   What are the main characteristics which contribute to an individual's decision to become an entrepreneur? Can these explain the variability in international levels of entrepreneurial activity or levels of entrepreneurial activity among men and women?
2   How do individuals' entrepreneurial decisions influence the institutional environment as envisaged in Figure 4.1? What are the specific mechanisms?
3   How would you explain the finding by Djankov *et al.* (2006) that shorter people were more likely to be entrepreneurs in Russia but taller people were more likely to be entrepreneurs in China?

Chapter 5

The start-up decision

5.1 INTRODUCTION

In this chapter we consider what influences the individual decision to actually start a business – to move from having an idea or seeing an opportunity to actually doing something about it. This is a big step for most people involving the commitment of significant time and, potentially, financial and reputational resources. It may also involve a potential loss of security if the potential entrepreneur has to give up a secure job to take a risk in starting a new firm (Box 5.1). In other situations the entrepreneurship decision may result from necessity due either to economic circumstances or losing a job.

Our interest in this chapter is to identify the range of factors which might shape the start-up decision. Is this solely about the individual, and potentially their family, or is it significantly influenced by other more institutional factors such as the availability of finance or social attitudes to enterprise or entrepreneurship? One recent study, for example, suggests that perceptions of the difficulty of accessing start-up finance discouraged potential entrepreneurs in the UK from starting businesses, an effect which was particularly strong for women (Roper and Scott, 2009). One interpretation is that this type of factor might help to explain the lower level of entrepreneurial activity among women in many countries. Other studies have emphasized the importance of legislation and regulation in the start-up process (Djankov *et al.*, 2002b, Capelleras *et al.*, 2008). In both cases there is a clear effect, both from individual psychology and attitudes and the operating environment on the start-up decision. Accordingly, it appears as if both structure and agency are likely to play key roles in the start-up decision.

The remainder of the chapter is organized as follows. In Section 5.2 we consider two different frameworks which have been used to reflect the start-up decision and which provide some information on the 'conversion ratio', the proportion of those individuals who think about entrepreneurship and then actually do it. Section 5.3 then focuses on three different approaches to the start-up decision from an economic, social and process perspective. Section 5.4 closes the chapter,

BOX 5.1 THE START-UP DECISION – INNOCENT DRINKS

Innocent Drinks is a UK-based company producing fruit drinks for the retail market. Richard Reed, one of the three co-founders of the company, relates how the decision to start the company was made:

> In the summer of 1998 when we had developed our first smoothie recipes but were still nervous about giving up our proper jobs, we bought £500 worth of fruit, turned it into smoothies and sold them from a stall at a little music festival in London. We put up a big sign saying 'Do you think we should give up our jobs to make these smoothies?' and put out a bin saying 'YES' and a bin saying 'NO' and asked people to put the empty bottle in the right bin. At the end of the weekend the 'YES' bin was full so we went in the next day and resigned.

Searching for start-up finance to establish the company turned out to be more difficult as the team was turned down 20 times by banks. Eventually the leadership team was backed by an American business angel. Today the company has sales in excess of around $220 million p.a.

Source: http://www.innocentdrinks.co.uk

integrating the start-up decision into the institutional model suggested by Lu and Tao (2010).

The main learning objectives for this chapter are as follows:

- To introduce students to economic, social and process-based theoretical perspectives on the start-up decision.
- To familiarize students with concepts of latent or nascent entrepreneurship and their measurement and their relationship to actual entrepreneurship.
- To encourage students to consider structure and agency and their interaction in the start-up decision.

Further questions for discussion and reading are outlined in Section 5.5.

5.2 THINKERS AND DOERS

The move from thinking about starting a business to actually starting up has received considerable attention in the research and policy literatures. The research literature has focused on the question of 'why' people make a particular start-up decision. The policy literature has also raised this question and has focused on trying to profile those who do and do not start businesses. In the UK, for example, a series of government surveys – the 'Household Survey of Entrepreneurship' – have tried to identify 'Thinkers', 'Doers' and 'Avoiders'. Doers are those adults who are self-employed or own a business. Thinkers are those who are not currently Doers, but have recently thought about starting a business, buying into an existing business or becoming self-employed. Avoiders are those who are neither Doers nor Thinkers. In the 2007 Household Survey of Entrepreneurship which covered 7,329 adults aged 16–64 across England, 14.3 per cent were Doers, 11.0 per cent were Thinkers and the remaining 74.7 per cent were Avoiders (IFF Research Ltd, 2008). The survey also provided some information about the type of factors which shape the barriers to either thinking about or starting a business (Figure 5.1). Issues related to finance and debt, a loss of security and the risk of the business failing were the key barriers to business start-up (Kihlstrom and Laffont, 1979). Very similar sets of barriers to start-up are evident in studies around the globe. Pillai and Amma (2005), for example, in a survey of women in India highlight very similar barriers to start-up: shortages of finance; lack of expert advice; lack of market outlets; shortage of raw materials/power; a lack of adequate training; conservative attitudes of society; and family responsibilities.

GEM – the Global Entrepreneurship Monitor – adopts slightly different names to cover essentially the same point, distinguishing between 'nascent' and 'actual'

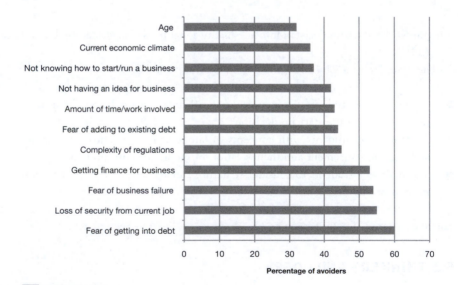

Figure 5.1
Barriers to starting a business: UK, 2007

Source: Adapted from IFF Research (2000), Chart 13.

entrepreneurs. Nascent entrepreneurs are those people who 'are actively committing resources to start a business that they expect to own themselves', but who have not yet started up a company (Bosma and Levie, 2010, p. 13). The higher the prevalence of nascent entrepreneurship the more 'dynamic' new firm activity in an economy is likely to be, and this can be measured by the percentage of the adult population who are nascent entrepreneurs (the nascent entrepreneurship activity rate or NEA). A second key factor is the 'conversion' of this nascent entrepreneurship into established business ownership. Here too the GEM data provide an easy indicator by relating the NEA to the overall proportion of the adult population in established business ownership (or established

Table 5.1 *Nascent and established entrepreneurship and conversion ratios – selected countries*

	Nascent entrepreneurship rate NEA (1) % adults	Established entrepreneurship activity EEA (2) % adults	Conversion ratio (2) × 100/(1)
Factor-driven economies			
Saudi Arabia	2.9	4.1	141.4
West Bank and Gaza	3.0	6.9	230.0
Syria	3.4	6.7	197.1
Venezuela	13.3	6.5	48.9
Guatemala	17.1	3.3	19.3
Yemen	22.8	2.9	12.7
Efficiency-driven economies			
Malaysia	1.7	4.3	252.9
Russia	1.8	2.3	127.8
Serbia	2.2	10.1	459.1
Chile	9.6	6.7	69.8
Colombia	15.0	12.6	84.0
Peru	16.1	7.5	46.6
Innovation-driven economies			
Denmark	1.6	4.7	293.8
Hong Kong	1.6	2.9	181.3
Italy	1.8	5.8	322.2
United States	4.9	5.9	120.4
Norway	5.0	8.3	166.0
United Arab Emirates	6.5	5.7	87.7
Iceland	7.6	8.9	117.1

Source: Derived from Bosma and Levie, 2010, Table 3, p. 21.

entrepreneurship activity rate or EEA). The ratio of the NEA to the EEA then provides a 'conversion' ratio: the higher the ratio the better an economy is at converting nascent into active entrepreneurship.

Based on data from the 2009 Global GEM Report, Table 5.1 summarizes the NEA, EEA and conversion rate data for selected countries. In Yemen, for example, 22.8 per cent of the adult population were categorized as Nascent Entrepreneurs in 2009 but established entrepreneurs were only 2.9 per cent of the adult population, suggesting a conversion ratio of only around 12.7 per cent. This suggests significant barriers to translating nascent entrepreneurship into business ownership compared to other countries such as Saudi Arabia or the West Bank and Gaza where the conversion ratio is much higher. More generally, conversion ratios are on average higher in the Innovation-driven economies (224.3 per cent), than in either the Efficiency-driven (162.4) or the Factor-driven economies (123.9 per cent) suggesting that Innovation-driven economies are better at converting nascent into actual entrepreneurship than those countries in the other two groups. Or, put another way, the barriers to moving into entrepreneurship are lower in the Innovation-driven economies than elsewhere.

5.3 CONCEPTUAL PERSPECTIVES

Three rather different conceptual perspectives on the start-up decision can be found in the literature. First, economic approaches emphasize business start-up as a labour market choice comparing the utility of start-up and working with little regard to the wider social or economic context within which individuals are located (Blanchflower and Oswald, 1998). Social approaches instead tend to emphasize the context and setting in which the start-up is taking place (van der Boon, 2005). Finally, process perspectives inject more temporality into the start-up decision process and emphasize the different stages of the decision process to move from 'Thinker' to 'Doer'.

Economic approaches to the start-up decision are perhaps best illustrated by a simplified version of the model outlined by Blanchflower and Oswald (1998). They suggest that an individual will choose to start a firm if their utility from taking this route is greater than their utility from working for someone else. The case of Rajeev Samant and the start-up of Sula Vineyards illustrates this type of decision (Box 5.2). To see how this model works at an economy-wide level Blanchflower and Oswald (1998) start by assuming that if an individual works for someone else their wage will be w and their utility is $u = w$. If, on the other hand, the individual starts a business they will have utility both from the profit of the enterprise and the non-financial benefits of being their own boss, say $u = \pi + i$, where π is the profit from the enterprise and i is the non-financial benefit of entrepreneurship. In the case of Rajeev Samant this non-financial benefit reflected both his preference

BOX 5.2 SULA VINEYARDS, INDIA

Rajeev Samant is a Stanford-trained engineer who worked as a finance manager at Oracle. In 1993, tired of corporate life in Silicon Valley, he moved back to India and took over his father's 28-acre rural estate near Nashik, 180 km northeast of Mumbai.

For four years Rajeev tried growing a range of different crops including organic mangoes, peanuts, roses and then table grapes, which were already common in the region. Then, a letter from a girlfriend provided the inspiration to start growing wine grapes and this led eventually to the establishment of Sula Vineyards. Seed capital for the business was provided by friends and family, and Kerry Damskey a winemaker from California's Sonoma Valley joined the company. Sula's first vines were planted in 1997 and today Sula is among India's most successful wine companies and has begun to develop associated tourist businesses.

Source: http://www.sulawines.com

for working in India and his desire to combine an element of working both in the city and the country.

If there is no start-up cost an individual will then start a firm if $\pi+i > w$, i.e. they would have greater utility from entrepreneurship than from working for someone else. To see how this works for the economy as a whole we need to make some assumptions about what determines π and w. Assume that there are a range of entrepreneurial opportunities in the economy offering different profit rates and that the more entrepreneurial ventures there are the lower the average profitability. This suggests that the returns to entrepreneurship will be downward sloping (Figure 5.2). Also, assume anyone can find work at wage w, or that the wage opportunities curve is horizontal (Figure 5.2). Taken together these suggest that if there is no cost of start-up, the equilibrium number of entrepreneurs will be at E1. To the left of this the returns to entrepreneurship are higher than the alternative wage, and to the right the returns are lower.

If there is a start-up cost, however, finance may be a significant barrier to start-up for many people as the survey data reviewed earlier suggest (Figure 5.1). If this is the case, Blanchflower and Oswald (1998) argue that the level of entrepreneurship may be constrained below the market equilibrium, say at E2. This involves a welfare loss. To test the importance of this financial barrier to the start-up decision Blanchflower and Oswald (1998) use longitudinal data from the UK's National Child Development Survey which covered all births from 3 to 9 March 1958 and surveyed children regularly thereafter. In this survey – like the UK Household Survey of Entrepreneurship discussed earlier (Figure 5.1) – the

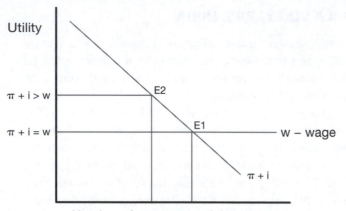

Number of entrepreneurial ventures

Figure 5.2
Utility-based model of the start-up decision

most commonly cited reason for people not becoming self-employed was the lack of capital and money. Blanchflower and Oswald (1998) found that receipt of an inheritance or gift had a positive effect on an individual becoming self-employed. This effect was larger for younger people, and provides further evidence of the significant effect of financial constraints on the start-up decision.

A key element of the economic approach to the start-up decision is that an individual can accurately evaluate the ensuing benefits. In practice, this is very unlikely to be the case and recent studies have emphasized the over-confidence of many potential entrepreneurs. As Townsend *et al.* (2010, p. 193) remark:

> hubris theory suggests that inflated expectations of success at the point of firm creation may contribute to subsequent failure in nascent firms as over-confident entrepreneurs start firms with insufficient capital, or over-allocate capital to high risk projects with little intrinsic chance of success.

Using data from the US Panel Study on Entrepreneurial Dynamics (PSED) Townsend *et al.* (2010) explore what aspects of this 'over-confidence' are important in shaping the probability of start-up. In particular, they explore whether it is potential entrepreneurs' expectations about the probability of the success of their enterprise or an overly positive view of their own entrepreneurial abilities which is more important in shaping the start-up decision. The empirical results emphasize individual assessment of one's own entrepreneurial ability as the most important determinant of the start-up decision. In other words, it is those who have the greatest self-belief who are most likely to make the most positive assessment of the returns to entrepreneurship and are therefore most likely to start businesses (see also Table 4.5).

An important critique of economic or utility approaches to the start-up decision is that they tend to be acontextual. Or, in other words, they tend to view the entrepreneurship decision in isolation from the context in which the decision is being made. In earlier chapters we have, however, emphasized the importance of context in the entrepreneurial decision, and the interaction between individual characteristics and the institutional context (McDade and Spring, 2005, Lu and Tao, 2010). The importance of the institutional context for entrepreneurship is reflected in more 'social' perspectives on the start-up decision which often focus on the combinations of factors which either 'pull' or 'push' individuals towards entrepreneurship. Van der Boon (2005, p. 163), for example, differentiates between these 'push' and 'pull' factors arguing that

> pull factors are those that pull an individual towards entrepreneur-ship, frequently said to include self-fulfilment, self-determination, a sense of accomplishment, control, profit . . . and family security . . . Push factors are those which push people out of their current jobs. . . . Being a victim of downsizing, having aspirations threatened, or women realizing they have hit the corporate glass ceiling.

The distinction between push and pull factors reflects, of course, the distinction between opportunity and necessity-based entrepreneurship discussed in earlier chapters. However, for many individuals the start-up decision may reflect a combination of 'push' and 'pull' factors; Caliendo and Kritikos (2008), for example, examine the start-up decision among 3,100 unemployed Germans whose start-ups were supported through two government enterprise support measures. From the sample, 83 per cent emphasized 'termination of employment' as key motive for start-up, with a further 35 per cent emphasizing the 'end of unem-ployment benefit entitlement'. Among the same group, 'pull' factors were also evident with 65 per cent of respondents having had their first customers and 56 per cent stating they had 'always wanted to be [their] own boss' (Caliendo and Kritikos, 2008, Table 5).

The study by Caliendo and Kritikos (2008) emphasizes the range of individual and institutional factors which can influence the start-up decision. It also suggests the temporal nature of the decision. Reflecting this, the third perspective on start-up emphasizes the temporal nature of the start-up decision seeing start-up as a process rather than a single event (Van de Ven and Engleman, 2004). It has been argued that process perspectives are useful as they highlight the different steps in the decision-making process moving towards enterprise and can provide insights

53

into the factors which influence the decision at different points in the start-up process. In terms of the earlier discussion (Section 5.2), for example, what factors influence the move from being an 'Avoider' to a 'Thinker' and from a 'Thinker' to a 'Doer'? Are these factors the same?

Some of the more detailed applications of the process perspective on the start-up decision stem from the US. Liao and Welsch (2008), for example, examine the range of different activities undertaken by US individuals starting technology- and non-technology-based enterprises. So, the process of establishing a new technology-based business was significantly longer than that for a non-technology-based business and it involved significantly more 'activities' such as seeking external finance, developing a business plan, etc. On a similar theme, Ndonzuau *et al.* (2002) develop a process or stage model of academic spin-outs. Based on an inductive or exploratory exercise which involved conversations with a group of staff in 15 universities recognized as having a record of success in promoting spin-out companies, they identify a four-stage process model of start-up. This highlights the very different support needs of academic entrepreneurs at different stages of the start-up process as well as the key issues which arise at each of the stages. The discussion in Ndonzuau *et al.* (2002) is summarized in Figure 5.3 emphasizing the initial ideas generation and finalization processes within the university and subsequent company growth and strengthening. For an illustration of the application of the Ndonzuau *et al.* model see Box 5.3.

Ideas generation	Finalize ideas	Company launch	Strengthening the firm
Activities Identification of research ideas with commercial potential	**Activities** Develop market proposition, proof of concept, prototyping, sourcing of finance	**Activities** Company formation, resource collation, venture team and network building	**Activities** Market building and development, organizational consolidation, innovation
Issues Academic culture Idea identification Idea evaluation	**Issues** Protection of ideas (IP) Technological evaluation/proving Commercial evaluation/proving	**Issues** Resource availability Management team Conflicts of interest Weak networks	**Issues** Resource availability Management team Growing pains Innovative capability
Inside university		**External to university**	

Figure 5.3
A process model of academic spin-outs

Source: Based on the discussion in Ndonzuau et al. (2002).

BOX 5.3 NOLDUS INFORMATION TECHNOLOGY

Lucas Noldus, the founder of Noldus Information Technology, was a PhD student at Wageningen University in the Netherlands. His research focused on the behaviour of wasps and led to the development of the initial version of 'The Observer', a software program for behavioural research (Ideas generation). Building on this prototype program, Noldus drew on the expertise and resources available in the university – office space and incubator facilities – to develop commercially saleable versions of the software and protect his IP (intellectual property). The university was also the first customer for the software, providing a validation of its value (Finalize ideas).

Noldus Information Technology was launched with support from Senter – a Dutch government agency with a mission to promote new technology-based firms. Government grants and technical subsidies also provided support for R&D and product development (Company launch). Profits recycled into the firm also provided resources for new software product development. This organic growth and reinvestment has continued and today the company employs around 100 people in Wageningen Science Park and sells a range of software and hardware products to 4,400 customers worldwide (Strengthening the firm).

Sources: http://www.noldus.com and Elfring and Hulsink (2003)

5.4 SUMMARY AND KEY POINTS

For most people the start-up decision marks the end, and perhaps also the beginning, of a process as they move towards becoming an entrepreneur or owner-manager. The empirical evidence suggests some commonality about the type of institutional factors which shape this process – finance, fear of failure, market opportunities – but also stresses the difference in the extent of these barriers towards entrepreneurship. In the less developed, Factor-driven economies, for example, the barriers to entrepreneurship – reflected in a lower conversion ratio – seem markedly greater than those in the Innovation-driven economies. While this may be enabling entrepreneurship to have more positive innovation, job creation and cohesion effects in the Innovation-driven economies (see Chapter 3), it remains the case that overall levels of both opportunity and necessity-driven entrepreneurial activity are higher in the Factor-driven economies.

Differences between countries in the barriers to entrepreneurship and the balance of opportunity and necessity-based entrepreneurial activity (or pull and

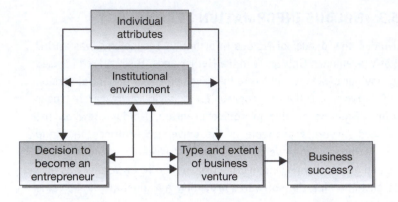

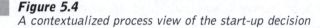

Figure 5.4
A contextualized process view of the start-up decision

push factors) again emphasize the contextual nature of entrepreneurship. In an international or comparative context this emphasizes the role of the institutional environment in shaping, and being shaped by, the entrepreneurship decision (McDade and Spring, 2005, Lu and Tao, 2010). Process models suggest, however, that the entrepreneurship decision itself may reflect a number of different 'activities'. Janice Langan-Fox (2005), for example, envisages a two-stage process in which individuals first choose to become an entrepreneur and second choose the type of business with which they get involved. Individual attributes and the institutional environment may shape both elements of the process suggesting the framework depicted in Figure 5.4.

Three features of this framework are perhaps worth highlighting. First, following Lu and Tao (2010) it links both individual attributes and the institutional environment to the entrepreneurial decision process, with institutional environment moderating the effects of individual attributes. Second, as suggested by McDade and Spring (2005), individual entrepreneurship decisions may themselves influence the institutional environment. Finally, it is worth reflecting that thus far we are only at the outset of the entrepreneurial journey. Subsequent chapters deal with the next stages.

5.5 DISCUSSION QUESTIONS AND FURTHER READING

Detailed data on nascent entrepreneurship in individual countries is available in the GEM Global reports for some years. The GEM model – see Bosma and Levie (2010) – also provides a structured framework within which nascent and actual entrepreneurship can be compared. For more depth on the different perspectives on the start-up decision see: on the economics, Blanchflower and Oswald (1998);

on the social perspective, Langan-Fox (2005); and on the process view Liao and Welsch (2008).

The start-up decision is strongly contextual and raises the following questions:

1 Issues related to finance and debt are often a major barrier to business start-up. Why is this? What are the implications of a shortage of start-up finance?
2 Which conceptual approach to the start-up decision is most helpful in explaining the start-up decision made by (a) Richard Reed (Box 5.1) and (b) Rajeev Samant (Box 5.2)?
3 In the process model of academic spin-outs (Figure 5.3) how does the type of support needed by the entrepreneur change through the different stages of the process? Think about this with reference to Noldus Information Technology (Box 5.3).

Chapter 6

Understanding business success: strategy, luck and policy

6.1 INTRODUCTION

Business success remains an enigma. Numerous studies have been undertaken over the years in an attempt to understand what determines business success, but attempts to conceptualize and statistically model this construct remain partial at best. In part this is easy to understand given the huge range of factors which can influence growth. Storey (1994), in his classic book on small business focuses, for example, on three main influences on small business performance – the background and characteristics of the entrepreneur or owner-manager, the nature of the business itself and the strategies adopted by the firm. Is this really the whole story, however, or, does this perspective over-emphasize factors internal to the business (Barkham et al., 1996)? Institutionalist perspectives discussed in previous chapters, for example, would also emphasize the organizational and regulatory context within which the firm is operating, suggesting that firms with similar entrepreneurial resources and characteristics might perform very differently in different national environments (Capelleras et al., 2008). Social networks may also be an important stimulus for growth, influencing the entrepreneur's ability to take advantage of market opportunities and external resources (Hoang and Antoncic, 2003, Zhao et al., 2010). Other studies have emphasized the role of market demand as a driver of business growth, suggesting the importance of business cycles and potentially public procurement (Piva and Vivarelli, 2007, Edler and Georghiou, 2007). A firm's location in a supportive entrepreneurial regional innovation system may also be a potential stimulus to entrepreneurship (Audretsch, 2005) and contribute to innovation and business growth (Roper et al., 2008).

Other issues surround the meaning of the term 'business success'. How is the performance of small firms best measured? Survival? Growth? Profitability? Coleman (2007), for example, considers the effects of human capital on both the growth and profitability of male- and female-owned businesses in the US. Morris *et al.* (2006) also review issues related to gender arguing that the growth orientation or ambition of male and female entrepreneurs may be different which, in turn, may have implications for business performance. More recently Hayter (2011) has examined the definitions of success which have been applied to university spin-out companies. This suggests an even broader range of success indicators including standard business performance measures as well as the scientific success of the venture (measured by patents and scientific papers) and the contribution of the venture to the success of the academic's university career. Three implications follow. First, in the majority of contexts the notion of business 'success' in entrepreneurial ventures is multi-dimensional reflecting more than simply standard business metrics such as growth or profitability. Second, measures of success are likely to depend on the specific attributes of the entrepreneurs themselves, and third – as in the case of the spin-outs discussed by Hayter – notions of 'success' are likely to be context-specific, again emphasizing the importance of a contextualized perspective on entrepreneurship and small business.

One dimension of small business performance which is relatively universal in most studies is growth, defined usually in terms of either sales or employment. For example, in their recent review of the development of research on international entrepreneurship Jones *et al.* (2011) emphasize the role of growth as a key strategic focus of 'born global' enterprises but also the centrality of measures of growth to the calibration of the success of international firms. Business growth also plays a central role in policy discussions and in terms of measuring the potential contribution of entrepreneurship and the small business sector to economic development (Ayyagari *et al.*, 2011). In subsequent sections of this chapter we therefore focus specifically on growth as a key indicator of business performance. As previous studies have suggested, however, the relationship between growth and other indicators of business performance is not always straightforward (Roper, 1999).

The remainder of the chapter is organized as follows. In Section 6.2 we review some of the empirical evidence on the international profile of business growth with a specific focus on high-growth and gazelle companies. This highlights the heterogeneity of firm growth rates in any period, the apparently rather random distribution of high-growth firms between sectors and the lack of persistence of above average growth rates. Each of these factors adds to the difficulties of developing effective models of growth and a range of conceptual and empirical approaches are reviewed in Section 6.3. At best, these deterministic models explain around 30 per cent of the variability in firm growth rates suggesting the potentially important role of luck in shaping business growth. Despite the difficulties in identifying its drivers, promoting business growth remains an important focus of enterprise policy and Section 6.4 considers the range of policy initiatives which have focused on supporting growing – and especially high-growth – businesses.

The key learning objectives of this chapter are:

■ To enhance students' understanding of the heterogeneity of firm performance and the difficulties this creates for developing understanding and predictive models.
■ To introduce recent evidence on the sectoral distribution of growth rates and a range of recent empirical and conceptual models including the impact of luck on business growth.
■ To explore why current models provide only a weak explanation of business growth.

Further discussion questions and reading are outlined in Section 6.6.

6.2 GROWTH, HIGH GROWTH AND GAZELLES

One of the main characteristics of business growth is its heterogeneity. In any period some firms grow very rapidly, others contract and many remain the same size. Some recent work for the UK provides a useful perspective on the distribution of growth rates within a population of firms. Anyadike-Danes *et al.* (2009) look at the distribution of employment growth rates of UK firms over the 2005 to 2008 period. The distribution is depicted in Figure 6.1 where we focus only on those firms with more than 10 employees. Around a third of firms with more than 10 employees maintained their employment over the 2005 to 2008 period, although around this growth rates varied widely. Significantly, around 9.9 per cent of firms lost more than 20 per cent of their employees over this three-year period.

Of equal interest are firms at the other end of the growth spectrum – those with high growth. But what do we actually mean by high growth? All types of definitions are possible but in recent work by the OECD a high-growth enterprise is defined as a firm with an 'average annualized growth in employees (or in turnover) greater than 20 per cent a year, over a three-year period, and with ten or more employees at the beginning of the observation period'. The share of high-growth enterprises can then be calculated as the number of high-growth enterprises as a percentage of the population of enterprises with ten or more employees (OECD, 2008b). In terms of the data presented by Anyadike-Danes *et al.* (2009), this means that in the UK around 5.8 per cent of firms would have been classified as 'high-growth' in the 2005 to 2008 period.

In the OECD data a group of young high-growth firms known as 'gazelles' are also defined. These are high-growth enterprises which are up to five years old and are of particular interest as a source of new jobs. Henrekson and Johansson (2010), for example, review twenty recent studies and conclude that 'a few rapidly growing firms generate a disproportionately large share of all net new jobs compared to non-high-growth firms. This is a clear-cut result' (Henrekson and

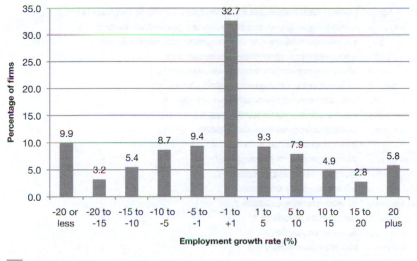

Figure 6.1
Distribution of growth rates of UK firms

Note: Based on firms with more than 10 employees.

Source: Adapted from Anyadike-Dones et al. (2009), Table A2, p. 42.

Johansson, 2010, p. 240). A crude rule of thumb, based on the evidence for different countries reviewed by Henrekson and Johansson (2010, Table 1) would suggest that around 4 per cent of firms – the gazelles – generally produce around half to three-quarters of all new jobs.

International data on high-growth firms and gazelles is available only for a relatively small group of OECD countries (Figures 6.2 and 6.3). The proportion of all firms in these countries which are 'high-growth' varies from 1.2 per cent in Romania to a high of 8.8 per cent in Bulgaria. In the US, around 5.5 per cent of firms meet the criteria for high growth (Figure 6.2). Proportions of gazelles are much lower, ranging from 0.1 per cent in the Netherlands to a high of 2.1 per cent in Bulgaria (Figure 6.3). Two key results stand out. First, high-growth firms represent only a small proportion – generally 5–10 per cent – of all small firms. Second, gazelles – young high-growth firms – are even rarer, accounting for only around 1–2 per cent of all small firms. Evidence from the OECD database also suggests that high-growth firms are also equally likely to occur in manufacturing and service sectors and are not particularly concentrated in high-tech sectors. Indeed, as Henrekson and Johansson (2010) note in their survey, gazelles are not over-represented in high-tech industries with a tendency instead to occur in services.

This OECD data provides information on the growth performance of established firms. Perhaps equally important, however, are the growth aspirations of entrepreneurs which have been shown to have a major impact on growth outcomes

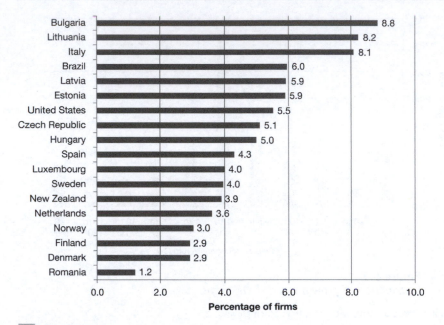

 Figure 6.2
Proportion of high-growth firms – selected OECD countries, 2005/6

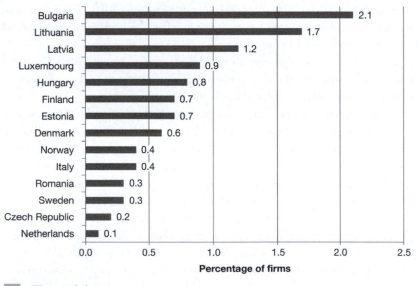

Figure 6.3
Proportion of gazelle firms – selected OECD countries, 2005/6

Note: Figures relate to the most recent year available for each country, either 2005 or 2006.

Source: OECD "Business Demography Indicators", Structural and Demographic Business Statistics (database). Accessed on 25 April 2011.

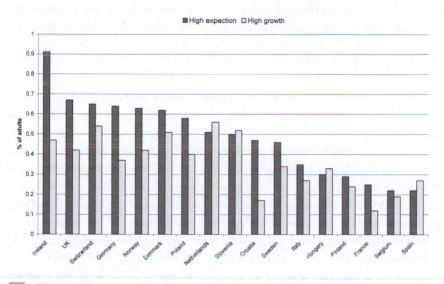

Figure 6.4

GEM indicators of high-expectation and high-growth entrepreneurs as a percentage of the adult population – selected countries

Source: GEM 2007 Report on high-growth entrepreneurship, Table 3, p. 22.

(Morris *et al.*, 2006). Here, as before, information is available from the Global Entrepreneurship Monitor (GEM) project. In GEM, 'high-expectation entrepreneurs' are those nascent and new entrepreneurs who expect to have more than 20 employees in five years (GEM, 2007), while 'high-growth entrepreneurs' are those who currently have 20 or more employees. The prevalence of high-expectation and high-growth entrepreneurs can both be expressed as a percentage of the adult population to give an indication of the general level of population engagement with 'high-growth' enterprise. In general terms across Europe, for example, between 0.2 and 0.9 per cent of the adult population report being engaged in high-expectation enterprise with a smaller – and more uniform percentage – engaged in high-growth firms (Figure 6.4).

6.3 UNDERSTANDING GROWTH

Two main conceptual perspectives on business growth dominate the research literature. In the tradition of organizational ecology the first focuses on the size distribution of firms within particular industries, and the underlying growth processes which the size distributions suggest (Cressy, 2006). For example, in 1931 Gibrat suggested his Law of Proportionate Growth, i.e. that a log-normal distribution of firm sizes could be explained if expected growth is proportional to firm size. In other words, if S is firm size, t a time indicator and ε a normally distributed error with mean zero and variance σ^2 Gibrat's law suggests that:

$$\log S_{t+1} = \log S_t + \varepsilon.$$

As Harrison (2004, p. 245) suggests, however, Gibrat's law faces several problems: it implies unbounded growth for some organizations and it fails to take into account factors such as mergers and acquisitions and the birth and death of organizations. More important perhaps are questions over whether the type of random growth process envisaged in Gibrat's law is actually capable of reproducing real world firm growth distributions which tend to have 'fat-tails' (Bottazzi et al., 2002). The implication is that growth is not purely a random process. Instead, something more systematic is going on. Jovanic (1982), for example, develops a model in which firm growth depends on entrepreneurial learning about the market, a model which is better able to predict the real shape of growth distributions than Gibrat's law. More recently Harrison (2004) simulates a range of different growth models which relate growth to firm size in different ways and tests their validity against a set of seven criteria. His conclusion is that: 'no generally applicable model of growth exists. Differences in the natures of industries and in firm strategies lead to different growth behaviours' (Harrison, 2004, p. 260). Or, in other words, business growth itself is context dependent.

Although this remains an area of active research interest (Bottazzi et al., 2011), Harrison's conclusion suggests the difficulty of identifying generalizations in terms of growth processes and suggests instead the potential importance of analysing growth determinants at the level of the individual firm. Two sorts of model are important here: Life-cycle or stage models, which view the life-cycle of the small business as a series of sequential states, and integrated or strategic models which adopt a more eclectic approach to explaining firm growth. Life-cycle models of business growth take various forms but generally envisage a series of growth 'stages' separated either by managerial or operational crises (Greiner, 1972) or changing resource requirements (Churchill, 2000, Xiao, 2011). Churchill (2000), for example, envisages six growth stages with firms growing from start-up through profitability to maturity. In practice, such models prove difficult to operationalize and often suggest the non-linearity and/or discontinuities in business development. Hanks et al. (1993), for example, explore the growth trajectory of 126 high-technology firms in the US state of Utah and use cluster analysis to identify six groups of firms which are depicted in Figure 6.5. Four of the clusters identified – start-up, expansion, maturity and diversification – fitted the development stages of the enterprise life-cycle model, with firms increasing in age and scale. The two other groups – lifestyle firms and capped growth – fell outside the linear growth trajectory envisaged in the linear life-cycle model and into what McMahon (2001) calls 'Disengagement Stages'. Together these groups accounted for 30 firms (23.6 per cent) of the total sample of 126. This illustrates one of the key critiques of life-cycle models – the implication that the business growth process is either linear or predictable. McMahon (2001) does suggest, however, that the Hanks *et al.* (1993) study and his own Australian data suggest the possibility of a conceptualization of business growth based on classifying firms into one of the six boxes in Figure 6.5.

The main alternative to the life-cycle type approach is an integrated or strategic approach which attempts to bring together the different drivers of business growth. Macpherson and Holt (2007) provide a recent review of the empirical evidence on small business growth and conclude: 'studies identify that the entrepreneur, the firm and the available social and business networks act as the mechanisms through which this is achieved (Box 6.1). Inevitably these three elements are not discrete' (p. 177). Wiklund *et al.* (2009) beginning at a similar starting point identify five sets of factors which have been shown to be important in previous growth studies:

■ entrepreneurial orientation which reflects a willingness to take risks, to innovate, as well as styles of management and control;

■ business environment which reflects market growth and dynamism and therefore the set of opportunities available to small firms;

■ strategic fit reflecting the extent to which the organization and structure of the firm is consistent with market needs;

■ resources such as finance, human capital, etc. but also including external resources accessed through partnerships, alliances or networks;

■ ambition, reflecting the commitment of the entrepreneur or leadership team to achieving growth.

Using Swedish survey data on 413 small firms from four sectors, Wiklund *et al.* (2009) conclude: 'the three constructs that have the strongest influence on growth are the growth attitude of the small business manager, the entrepreneurial orientation of the firm and the dynamism of the task environment where the firm operates' (Wiklund *et al.*, 2009, p. 367). Overall, their model is able to explain around 30 per cent of the variation in growth rates in their sample. This type of result is not uncommon. In their recent paper on Chinese firms, for example, Zhao *et al.* (2010) are able to explain around a quarter of the variance in firm growth rates. In UK studies, even with relatively complex models, we obtain similar results, explaining 10–15 per cent of the variability of business growth (Mole *et al.*, 2008a, 2008b). Why are such models so poor at explaining the variation in growth rates between firms?

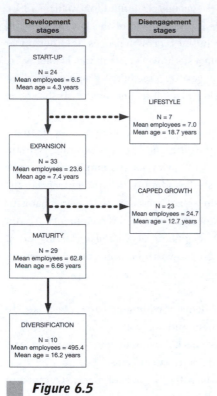

Figure 6.5
Applying the enterprise lifestyle model

Source: Adapted from McMahon (2001), Figure 1, and Hanks et al. (1993).

Two potential explanations are possible. First, it could simply be that the variables we are using to capture or explain growth are themselves inadequate. Second, and perhaps more likely, it could be that we have an omitted variable – such as luck. Parnell and Dent (2009), for example, suggest that studies of business performance reflect one of three perspectives. First, in some studies growth processes are seen as essentially deterministic – firms with specific characteristics or resources will grow at the same rate. This perspective is implicit in studies in the positivist, econometric tradition which implicitly assume that luck plays no systematic role in the growth process, with growth instead being determined by observable characteristics (Barkham *et al.*, 1996, Mole *et al.*, 2008b). Second, luck may be seen as potentially important in influencing business growth in the short term but has no long-term effect. In econometric models of business performance this interprets luck as 'noise' or measurement error and is captured in error terms in the model. Parnell and Dent (2009) highlight a third rather persuasive perspective, however, which suggests that luck may have more persistent performance effects generating either positive or negative path dependence

BOX 6.1 HIGH-GROWTH FIRMS IN AFRICA

Little robust evidence exists on the drivers of high-growth firms in the developing and low-income economies of sub-Saharan Africa. An exception is a recent study based on the OECD definitions of high-growth firms and gazelles and covering 954 firms taken from the World Bank Investment Climate Survey. This analysis explores both the determinants of growth and the determinants of the distribution of growth rates. Following the general practice in integrated or strategic models of growth, explanatory factors include firm size and age, innovation, the characteristics of the entrepreneur and firms' internal resources. Three key results emerge. First, innovating firms are significantly more likely to be in the high-growth category than non-innovating firms. Second, transport costs and availability are key determinants of growth as is the educational level of entrepreneurs and their workforce. Third, other factors such as training have a compressing effect on the distribution of growth rates rather than increasing average growth rates. Overall, models explain between 7 and 29 per cent of the variance in company growth rates.

Source: Goedhuys and Sleuwaegen (2010)

(Barney, 1986). Lucky entrepreneurs, for example, may be able to invest more in future products or services generating greater future success. Short-term luck then becomes long-term success. None of the models of small business performance we have reviewed take this potentially important driver of growth into account.

6.4 POLICY SUPPORT FOR BUSINESS GROWTH

The importance of high-growth firms and gazelles in creating new jobs – something which is widely recognized by policy-makers around the world – means that this type of firm has become an important focus of policy. The key question is what can be done to maximize growth and make a contribution to national growth and competitiveness. Is it possible to identify certain types of enterprises or entrepreneurs which are most likely to achieve high growth? Or, is luck so important that it is impossible to pick winners? Are firms in high-tech sectors a better bet than those in low-tech or more traditional sectors? Are well-educated entrepreneurs more likely to establish fast growing firms? Or, is it better for governments to focus on developing the institutional environment within which all small firms can grow?

67

In fact, the policy problem posed by high-growth firms is even more difficult than the rarity of high-growth firms and gazelles noted earlier actually suggests. The key issue is whether a firm which achieves high growth in one period will actually continue to achieve high growth. In other words is high growth persistent? Parker *et al.* (2010, p. 223), for example, investigate the growth profile of a group of 100 high-growth UK firms which achieved mean sales growth of 36 per cent p.a. between 1992 and 1996 and conclude: 'surviving gazelles grew by just 8 per cent between 1996 and 2001. Thus, gazelle-like growth appears to be fragile, having failed to persist over a decade, even in a period of impressive macro-economic growth.' Based on a broader analysis of all UK firms, Anyadike-Danes *et al.* (2009) reach an essentially similar conclusion: 'Not only was the experience of high-growth relatively rare, but multiple instances were even rarer, affecting only one-third of high-growth firms' (Anyadike-Danes *et al.*, 2009, p. 31). For policy-makers, both the rarity and lack of persistence of high growth create difficult issues of policy design and targeting.

Efforts to support business growth come in different forms. Web-based portals such as Singapore's 'EnterpriseOne' (http://www.business.gov.sg) provide an initial point of information and access to government services while specialist support agencies such as Catalonia's ACC10 provide services to individual firms to support their growth and development (Box 6.2). Other types of support institutions such as business incubators have also developed to support start-up development and tackle problems associated with lack of capital, poor management and insufficient market understanding. In general terms, business incubators provide rentable office and/or factory space for new ventures during their early years. Typically 'the role of business incubators is to provide a supportive environment, where new entrepreneurs receive training and assistance in business management and marketing, various other business services, and access to seed capital' (Avnimelech *et al.*, 2007, p. 1185). It has been suggested that incubators add value to their tenants in four areas: diagnosing business needs, selecting and monitoring their tenants, providing access to business networks and providing access to capital. It has also been suggested that incubators may enhance the entrepreneurial culture of an area and act as a magnet for highly skilled individuals looking to benefit from the services provided by the incubator. Analyses of the Israeli incubator network suggest that this attractor effect of incubators may work even in rural and peripheral areas. This effect may be deceptive, however, as the same study also suggests that the subsequent success rate of firms attracted may then be relatively low (Avnimelech *et al.*, 2007).

Two key success factors emerge from the incubator literature. First, the geographic context in which the incubator is located is a very significant influence on its success (Box 6.3). In the Israeli case, for example, research has shown that incubator success rates increase sharply where they are closely related to venture capital provision (Avnimelech *et al.*, 2007). Second, the evidence suggests that the

BOX 6.2 ACC10, BARCELONA

ACC10 is a publicly funded organization which delivers a wide range of business support measures on behalf of the Catalan Ministry of Innovation, Universities and Enterprise. The aim of the organization is to make Catalonia a leading economy in the global market by providing Catalan businesses with a competitive edge. Its mission is

- to increase business productivity by improving three main factors: innovation, technology and talent;
- to promote the value of the products and services of Catalan companies in international markets;
- to increase the number of Catalan companies and products in international markets.

ACC10 employs around 300 people in total: around 220 in the main office in Barcelona and around 80 in a network of 35 international offices. ACC10 is also a member of the Enterprise Europe Network (EEN).

ACC10 has a front office which provides the initial point of contact with firms. Enquiries are then routed to specialist servicers within the organization. A high quality customer relations management system provides information on current and past client interactions and ensures coordination of support. Key types of support relate to measures to support internationalization, R&D and innovation. This includes support to help small firms to engage in international partnerships and procurement initiatives.

Sources: Interview with ACC10 staff, http://www.acc10.cat/en/catalonia-barcelona; and http://www.enterprise-europe-network.ec.europa.eu

management and operation of the incubator itself can also be a significant determinant of its success with different forms of incubation service adding value to different types of company (Duff, 1994). In Jyväskylä Science Park in Finland, for example, the regional development company has developed parallel incubator and light-touch mentoring (company-clinic) approaches for high-growth firms with different needs (see Box 6.4).

Many incubators are located close to universities or on science parks and a range of other related policy initiatives have also developed to support the development of entrepreneurship among graduates and the commercialization of university research. In some cases these have involved changes to the operation and organization of universities, and changes in the way universities engage and cooperate with businesses. This reflects the emphasis on interaction and co-operation in the discussion of the entrepreneurial regional innovation system in Chapter 2 (Cooke and Leydesdorff, 2006). There has been some focus upon the role of the 'entrepreneurial university' in the regional innovation system. Here, students are encouraged to participate in enterprise activity and placements, and there is close relationship between faculty, entrepreneurship educators and

BOX 6.3 BUSINESS INCUBATION IN SOUTH AFRICA

Buys and Mbewana (2007) report an analysis of the Godisa incubators in South Africa. Business incubation was first introduced in South Africa in 1995 and the Godisa initiative, which included 12 business incubators spread across South Africa, was launched in 2000 by the departments of Trade and Industry and of Science and Technology. The aim of the Godisa Programme has been to create technology-intensive small, medium and micro enterprises through the enhancement of technological innovation, improvement in productivity and accelerated international competitiveness.

Based on a questionnaire survey covering programme managers, incubator managers and entrepreneurs eight key success factors are identified:

■ access to science and technology expertise and facilities;
■ availability of funding;
■ quality of entrepreneurs;
■ stakeholder support;
■ supportive government policies;
■ competent and motivated incubator management;
■ financial sustainability; and
■ networking.

Buys and Mbewana (2007) conclude

> that the Godisa case study shows that incubators that operate in conducive environments tend to be the most successful. . . . Conducive environments for business incubation are located where access to scientific and technical knowledge and services and supporting infrastructure is readily available (p. 358).

Source: Buys and Mbewana (2007)

BOX 6.4 INCUBATION AND LIGHT-TOUCH MENTORING, JYVÄSKYLÄ SCIENCE PARK, FINLAND

A systemic approach to business incubation has been developed in Jyväskylä Science Park, Finland since the first incubation facilities were offered in 1992. This involves a combination of formal incubator and other light-touch provision.

The formal incubation process includes both pre-incubator and post-incubator phases where assistance and counselling are offered to firms. The pre-incubator phase represents the planning phase for business operations. Together with expert personnel from the business incubator, the future entrepreneur prepares a business plan for the company. It takes two to six months before a business plan (including a cash flow estimate for one year and budget planning for three years) is ready. During this period the future entrepreneur has access to the well developed and tested budget and production planning tools of the business incubator.

Companies that successfully pass the pre-incubation period are allowed up to two years in the incubator. As a principle, premises and facilities are negotiated individually with each company, and the agreement also foresees business consulting services and individual counselling for the incubation period.

The post-incubation phase consists of a mentoring service that is offered for the company. The mentor advises the company and helps find business-related solutions. The mentor can serve as adviser to the company, outside adviser to the board or as a member of the board.

In addition to the physical incubator space, the Jyväskylä Regional Development Company Jykes Ltd, has developed a 'light-touch' company-clinic service targeted at companies working in the field of knowledge-intensive business services. This does not provide physical incubator space but delivers consulting advice to help firms identify specific barriers to the survival and growth of participant companies. The services are also aimed at helping companies to better plan and manage their growth, which is of great relevance for growth-oriented companies. On a needs basis, tools to enhance the company's capacities and capabilities are developed.

Source: Discussion Paper. 'Entrepreneurship in the Districts Mittweida and Altenburger Land', OECD LEED Programme in *OECD LEED Local Entrepreneurship Series*, October 2006

entrepreneurs (NESTA, 2008). Other writers have emphasized how universities have moved from a traditional 'open science' model, where new knowledge is viewed as a public good, towards more careful control of new intellectual property (EU, 2004). In the traditional 'open science' model, universities essentially adopt a passive approach to intellectual property (IP) development and exploitation with commercialization depending on the take-up of new technologies by firms. More recently, however, and most notably in the United States since the Bayh-Dole Act, universities and public research organizations have placed increasing emphasis on their private ownership of IP and consequently have had the incentive to adopt a more proactive role in IP development and exploitation. This gives rise to the licensing model (EU, 2004). Here, universities engage in basic research but are proactive; they devote resources to the identification, development and subsequent exploitation of IP, generally through patents and licensing. The EU believes that this approach can generate substantial benefits, 'It is estimated that at least half the new products based on university patents would not have been developed if the results had been put in the public domain without patent protection' (p. 11).

Mowery *et al.* (2004) argue that the increased focus on the commercialization of university research has, however, at least in the United States, gone beyond the licensing model, influencing the nature of university research itself. This has 'changed the research culture of US universities, leading to increased secrecy, less sharing of research results, and a shift in the focus of academic research away from fundamental towards more applied topics' (p. 1). In this 'innovation model', universities both adopt a proactive approach to IP development and exploitation *and* re-orient the type of R&D they are undertaking to bridge the gap between fundamental university research and its commercialization.

The University of Waterloo situated at the heart of Canada's Technology Triangle provides an outstanding example of an entrepreneurial university and, arguably, a university which has embraced the innovation model (Bramwell and Wolfe, 2008). Strongly embedded within the regional community, dense co-operative networks on technology and enterprise between the university and the local community are complemented by the university's cooperative education programme. 'The rotation of students to industry and back to the classroom solidified already tight relations with local industry. The reflexive relationship has allowed the curriculum to keep up with the ever changing technological frontiers of industry' (Bramwell *et al.*, 2008, p. 105). Over 250 spin-outs from the university have resulted in part from the university policy of allowing ownership of intellectual property to rest with its creator (faculty or student), encouraging both creativity and enterprise.

A key element of the success of the University of Waterloo in establishing itself as an entrepreneurial university has been its strong relationships with business organizations in the region (Bramwell and Wolfe, 2008). This contrasts strongly with some other regions where the research orientation of the universities has a weaker link to the needs of local firms (Roper *et al.*, 2006). Identifying institutional mechanisms to promote coherence between the research focus of universities and the needs of local businesses has proved difficult although recent experience with so-called Competence Research Centres (CRCs) has been positive. CRCs bring together enterprises and research centres in a long-term collaborative relationship aimed at a particular technology under independent governance arrangements. The best established network of CRCs (in Sweden) has provided strong evidence of the value of this type of initiative, a result echoed in early evaluation results from Hungary and Estonia (see Box 6.5). In recent years, CRCs have also been seen as playing a significant role in internationalization and SME development. CRCs often act as a focal point or gateway for international R&D collaboration, and their relatively high profile can provide an attraction for SME participation.

6.5 SUMMARY AND KEY POINTS

The question of what determines business success remains, at this point, unanswerable in any statistically robust sense. Models in the literature explain less than a third of the variation in firm growth rates, for example, with the remaining two-thirds of the variation in growth rates unexplained. This poses a significant challenge for those researching in this area as well as for policy-makers trying to understand the growth process and develop relevant policy instruments. Business growth or success – like the earlier stages of the entrepreneurial journey – also emerges as strongly contextual. Again, institutions matter, suggesting that explanations of success based solely on firm-specific (or entrepreneur-specific) factors are unlikely to be effective. As Macpherson and Holt (2007) suggest, for example, social and business networks may be an important driver of business growth and the growth effect of these is likely to interact with, or at least be moderated by, the characteristics of the individual entrepreneur or owner-manager. Studies such as that by Wiklund *et al.* (2009) also emphasize the role of entrepreneurial orientation and aspiration and strategy in shaping business growth. Building on these studies and the arguments developed in the previous chapters (see Figure 5.4), this suggests the research framework depicted in Figure 6.6.

Here of course, the specific individual attributes and aspects of the business environment which might be relevant to shaping the entrepreneurial decision, the type of enterprise and business strategy may be very different (Rauch and Frese, 2007). Earlier chapters have focused on the attributes of the entrepreneur; in the next two chapters we focus on two of the most frequently identified firm-specific factors linked to growth – finance and innovation.

BOX 6.5 COMPETENCE RESEARCH CENTRES: LINKING RESEARCH AND INNOVATION

Modelled on the Engineering Research Centres set up in the United States in the mid-1980s, Competence Research Centres (CRCs) have been successfully established in a number of European countries since 1995. Among the most recently established networks of CRCs have been the KKK Competence Centres established in 2000 in Hungary and Competence Centres established in Estonia in 2003.

According to the COMPERA ERA-Net network a CRC is a 'structured, long-term R&D collaboration in a strategically important area between academia, industry and the public sector. The aim is to bridge the gap between scientific and economic innovation by providing a collective environment.' Typically CRCs concentrate on a specific technological area and have some long-term (e.g. ten-year) public funding. In general CRCs comprise a university-based research facility undertaking collaborative research with a network of partner firms.

The longest established European CRCs are the Swedish Competence Centres which were established in 1995 and evaluated in detail in 2003. The evaluation concluded

> the Swedish competence centres programme is a relevant and effective instrument that builds the people and networks needed for industrial competitiveness, tunes universities towards socio-economic needs . . . and produces significant social and economic value . . . In sum: the argument for competence centres is overwhelming.

Key impacts were identified in knowledge creation, upgrading research skills, extended networks, innovation and attracting inward investment.

Sources: Vinnova (2004), *Impacts of the Swedish Competence Centres Programme 1995–2003*. VA 2004: 03. Available at: http://www.vinnova.se; Monteny, F (2008) 'COMPERA – Some Experiences', presentation to the Compera Workshop on CRCs, Dusseldorf, February 2009

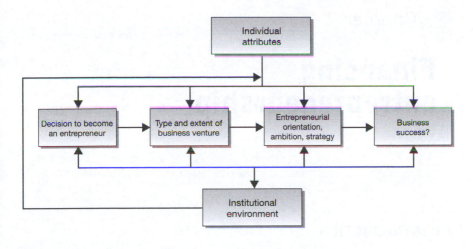

Figure 6.6
Contextualized view of business start-up and success

6.6 DISCUSSION QUESTIONS AND FURTHER READING

Storey (2011) provides a useful description of the current state of the art in terms of understanding business growth and a thought-provoking critique of current models. Parnell and Dent (2009) more broadly provide a discussion of the lack of any treatment of luck in managerial theory and by implication in discussions of small business growth. Different studies then emphasize different drivers of growth: on human resources see Coleman (2007) and on networks see Hoang and Antoncic (2003). Goedhuys and Sleuwaegen (2010) provide an interesting alternative perspective using quantile regression techniques.

The following discussion questions are suggested:

1　What factors explain the wide variation in firm growth rates noted by Anyadike-Danes *et al.* (2009)? Is growth purely random?
2　How important is the role of luck in explaining business growth? Can this explain why models of small business growth have such low levels of explanatory power?
3　What policy initiatives could be taken to support business growth? Would you target gazelles or slower growing firms?

Chapter 7

Financing entrepreneurship

7.1 INTRODUCTION

Obtaining appropriate finance is a fundamental issue for all businesses whatever their location and whether they are opportunity- or necessity-based. Indeed, an almost ubiquitous finding of business surveys which explore the barriers to start-up and growth is the importance of either shortages or the cost of finance (Fraser, 2005, Pillai and Amma, 2005). In more developed economies with well-developed financial and legal institutions, attention has often focused on funding 'gaps' although attention has also focused on discouraged borrowers (Kon and Storey, 2003) and the lack of investment readiness of some firms. In less developed and transition economies, funding issues may also reflect weaknesses on both the supply and demand sides (Levitsky and Prasad, 1989, Duan *et al.*, 2009). Supply-side weaknesses may reflect a simple lack of supply of finance due to a paucity of lending institutions, or a preference for lending to larger borrowers. Demand-side weaknesses may reflect a lack of collateral or the higher risks entrepreneurs pose to lenders. In either case, policy initiatives have developed to counter these issues focused often on reducing the risk of lending and increasing the supply of loan capital to entrepreneurs and SMEs through credit guarantee schemes.

In recent years traditional funding mechanisms have also been challenged by the growth of alternative funding approaches which have extended the supply of available finance. Islamic banking, for example, provides an alternative and for some, more acceptable, form of business finance (Obaidullah and Latiff, 2008). Micro-finance or micro-credit schemes have also made funding available for the first time to marginalized communities in both developing and, increasingly, developed economies. Both forms of finance have the potential to enhance individuals' ability to move into entrepreneurship and are considered later in the chapter. Before considering these, however, Section 7.2 reviews the evidence on the use of alternative funding sources by small firms across the globe and highlights the generality of concerns about access to finance. Section 7.3 focuses on policy and regulatory steps which have been taken in different countries to broaden firms' access to finance, focusing on the rapid growth in recent years of credit guarantee schemes. Islamic finance is the focus of Section 7.4.

The main learning objectives for this chapter are as follows:

- To introduce students to the main sources of entrepreneurial finance and how the use of these differs around the world. Institutional explanations will be explored.
- To help students to critically evaluate the main conceptual explanations which have been advanced to explain entrepreneurs' funding choices.
- To introduce students to the main principles of Islamic finance and to explore the consequences for entrepreneurship.

Further reading and questions for discussion are given in Section 7.6.

7.2 SME FUNDING – THE GLOBAL PICTURE

Fundamental to any understanding of the global pattern of entrepreneurial finance are the distinctions between internal and external financing, and between debt and equity. Typically 'internal' funding is thought to consist of the entrepreneur's own or family resources or the retained profits from the current or prior enterprises. 'External' funding includes both equity and debt financing. Debt financing typically involves loan finance from a bank or credit institution with a fixed duration and rate of interest. Such loans may be short-term, intended to cover working capital or specific transactions, or long-term to finance investment in premises or equipment. In either case, lenders may require collateral, which may limit the accessibility of debt finance to smaller or newer firms. Private equity finance on the other hand – typically associated with venture capital or business angel funding – involves sharing business ownership as well as any associated profits and losses. Public equity also involves sharing ownership where firms are publicly quoted. Growing firms often make use of a range of different types of finance as they grow and develop, often moving from internal finance through debt or equity funding (Box 7.1).

While these distinctions – internal vs. external, debt vs. equity – are perhaps the most fundamental differences between the types of finance used by small firms, the actual mix of funding used by small firms varies widely between countries. Beck *et al.* (2008a), for example, report an analysis of the World Business Environment Survey undertaken in 1999 which considers the proportion of external finance (from banks, equity partners, etc.) used by firms in a wide range of countries. The survey data are dominated by smaller firms and so they argue that they can be interpreted as reflecting the funding mix used by small firms. Focusing on the proportion of external funding, their data suggest that in many countries, including some developed economies (e.g. France, the UK), the

BOX 7.1 FINANCING FOOTFALL

John Gallagher and his business partner started developing systems to monitor the flow of customers – or 'footfall' – in shopping centres in 1989. Working from home, the partners developed and sold video-based systems. A $400,000 contract with a Spanish shopping group suggested the potential value of the business and led to an investment of $160,000 from three business angels. By 2004, the company had a turnover of $10.9 million p.a, an annual growth rate of 60–70 per cent, and a UK market share of 80 per cent. At this point the business model involved selling hardware and software packages to customers and then providing periodic maintenance. John Gallagher remarked: 'Our clients were telling us their biggest problem was data quality, while ours was continuous revenue generation'.

Footfall's solution was to change the business model to provide customers with a data service for a monthly fee rather than selling hardware packages. Moving to this business model, however, required both a change in strategic direction and additional investment. Footfall's original angel investors were uncomfortable on both counts. 'Why' they asked 'change a business model which remains profitable, and why dilute their shares in the business?' Additional venture capital investment of $7.8 million was made in the company before its sale to Experian in 2005. This 'exit' allowed the firm's venture capital investors and the owners to release their own investments.

Sources: *Birmingham Post,* 23 June 2004 and 6 January 2006

majority of small business funding remains internal, while in some transition economies (e.g. Armenia, Belarus) internal funding accounts for as much as 90 per cent of business funding (Table 7.1). This is likely to relate primarily to supply-side conditions and the relative under-development of the commercial banking sector in such economies. After analysing the effect of business size and other factors on the use of external finance by firms Beck *et al.* (2008a, p. 485) conclude that:

> Small firms use less external finance, especially bank finance. But small firms also benefit the most from better protection of property rights and financial intermediary development . . . Thus, the most effective way of improving small firm access to external finance appears to be through institutional reforms addressing the weaknesses in legal and financial systems.

Table 7.1 *Proportion of business finance from external sources – selected countries*

	% external			% external
Italy	77.7		Spain	39.8
Estonia	60.1		Lithuania	39.6
Poland	58.6		Slovenia	38.6
Chile	57.3		United Kingdom	36.1
Nicaragua	56.7		Hungary	35.9
Germany	54.3		Peru	35.5
Uruguay	54.0		Czech Republic	32.5
Brazil	51.8		France	30.9
United States	47.1		China	29.9
Singapore	45.2		Venezuela	28.7
Turkey	44.0		Romania	25.9
Argentina	43.5		Haiti	24.2
Pakistan	43.1		Belarus	20.4
Malaysia	40.6		Armenia	11.4

Source: Beck et al. (2008).

Accessing appropriate finance remains an issue for many small firms. Even in countries where the banking sector is well developed it is widely recognized that SMEs often face difficulties in obtaining finance. Four main reasons for this have been suggested (Levitsky and Prasad, 1989, Duan *et al.*, 2009). First, lending to entrepreneurs or SMEs may carry higher risks than lending to larger or more established firms. Reflecting the 'liability of newness', small firms generally have higher mortality rates than larger companies and may be more vulnerable to market and economic changes (Coleman, 2004). Second, banks and financial institutions may be institutionally biased towards lending to large corporate borrowers. This may reflect prior relationships – joint directorships, track record, etc. – or simply banks' preference for prestige clients. Third, transaction costs are likely to be proportionally higher on the relatively small loans required by entrepreneurs or SMEs. This is likely to reduce the profitability of this type of lending and its attractiveness to finance institutions. Finally, SMEs seeking loans may be unable or unwilling to provide accounting records, securities or collateral for loans. This may – either unintentionally or intentionally – create informational asymmetries which make it difficult for lenders to accurately assess lending risk.

It has been suggested that in developing or transition economies these four obstacles to SME financing may be exacerbated by a range of other institutional and legal issues (Allen and Udell, 2006):

■ The banking sector may be highly concentrated and uncompetitive, encouraging banks to adopt conservative lending policies and/or charge high interest rates. In this situation banks may have little incentive to lend to SMEs.

■ Insufficiently developed legal systems may prevent the use of some forms of financing instrument. Legal provisions regarding security interests may for example determine the potential value of collateral. Similarly, depending on how the legal system protects minority shareholders, venture capital or angel financing may be reduced.

■ Enforcement difficulties may also create significant disincentives to invest. Appropriate regulatory frameworks may be in place (e.g. cadasters or registers of movable assets) but potentially lengthy legal proceedings and corruption may discourage investment.

■ Informational infrastructure (credit bureaus, sources of information on payment performance) may also be limited.

Table 7.2, for example, reports data taken from the World Bank Enterprise Surveys which record the percentage of small firms identifying access to finance as a major difficulty in 2008 or 2009 in a group of African economies. On average in these countries nearly half of the firms surveyed (48.3 per cent) reported that finance was a major difficulty, around three times the proportion of small firms emphasizing finance as a difficulty in the same survey in Germany (2005, 16.3 per cent) and India (2006, 17.0 per cent). Even within this group of African countries,

Table 7.2 *Proportion of firms reporting access to finance as a major difficulty – selected African countries, 2009/10*

	% Firms experiencing difficulty obtaining finance
Angola	39.4
Benin	69.9
Botswana	35.2
Congo	43.1
Gabon	34.3
Ivory Coast	75.6
Lesotho	32.4
Liberia	34.8
Malawi	64.4
Niger	61.2
Sierra Leone	40.5
Average	48.3

Source: Author's analysis of World Bank Enterprise Surveys.

access to finance varies widely, with firms in the Ivory Coast nearly twice as likely to report difficulties accessing finance than those in Botswana or Gabon (Table 7.2). It is also worth noting that the approach adopted in the Enterprise Surveys means that these figures are likely to reflect views of legally operating, formally constituted companies. The figures are therefore likely to *underestimate* the difficulty of informal enterprises in obtaining external finance.

Some countries have, however, been able to make significant progress in strengthening their institutional systems over the last decade with a resulting decline in the proportion of firms citing finance as a major difficulty. In Bulgaria, for example, data from successive World Bank Enterprise Surveys suggests that the proportion of firms highlighting finance difficulties nearly halved over the 2002 to 2005 period with a similar improvement in Bosnia and Herzegovina (Table 7.3). More recently, however, the situation has again deteriorated in some countries with data collected during 2008 and 2009 emphasizing firms' difficulty in accessing finance during the recession.

Table 7.3 *Proportion of firms reporting access to finance as a major difficulty – selected European countries, 2002, 2005 and 2008/9*

	2002 % firms	2005 % firms	2008/9 % firms	Average % firms
Armenia	24.4	15.3	34.0	24.6
Azerbaijan	9.2	10.9	30.5	16.9
Belarus	27.0	29.9	39.1	32.0
Bosnia and Herzegovina	25.6	15.2	29.1	23.3
Bulgaria	45.6	20.2	18.3	28.0
Czech Republic	30.4	29.5	23.7	27.9
Estonia	12.5	8.6	8.7	9.9
Georgia	10.7	24.1	40.8	25.2
Kyrgyzstan	11.4	14.3	22.7	16.1
Lithuania	11.1	7.3	24.5	14.3
Macedonia	13.3	20.6	33.1	22.3
Moldova	31.3		36.1	33.7
Poland	42.3	36.3	25.0	34.5
Romania	36.5	22.6	41.1	33.4
Russia	19.0	14.9	42.5	25.5
Slovenia	13.3	17.7	13.2	14.8
Tajikistan	17.8	4.9	24.4	15.7
Ukraine	27.0	24.7	35.1	28.9
Uzbekistan	30.7	12.1	22.9	21.9
Average	23.1	18.3	28.7	23.4

Source: Author's analysis of World Bank Enterprise Surveys.

The difficulties faced by many firms in accessing finance in transition and developing economies raise profound implications for growth and development, and the capability of entrepreneurship to deliver the benefits of job creation, innovation and social cohesion outlined in Chapter 3. These difficulties also make clear the limited circumstances in which standard theoretical models are helpful in explaining funding choices. For example, in the literatures on business finance in Europe and the US, pecking order models are often discussed (Vanacker and Manigart, 2010). Here, the basic idea is that entrepreneurs or small business owner-managers have a preference for alternative sorts of funding depending on their perception of the relative risks and rewards. Debt funding, for example, allows the firm to capture more of any upside returns than equity. Equity funding – such as funding from business angels or venture capital firms – may have other benefits aside from finance, however. For firms in high-tech sectors, for example, receiving equity investments may send positive signals to other potential funders or customers about the quality of a firm (Hogan and Hutson, 2004). There is substantial evidence from more developed countries suggesting the validity of the pecking order hypothesis. Howarth (2001), for example, describes qualitative evidence from UK firm owners regarding their funding preferences; this indicated an unwillingness to share the ownership of the firms and, accordingly, a preference for debt rather than equity funding. Typical comments were:

> We do have an aversion to external finance . . . I don't see why I should pay the bank out of our profit margins . . . It's mine and I want it to stay all mine.

> They want equity and I don't want anybody to have an interest in the company other than myself.

> Hell freezing over describes the likelihood of us seeking outside funding.

Recent evidence from high-growth companies confirms the preference in more developed countries for internal funding but also emphasizes the potential importance of equity financing in helping firms to grow more rapidly than a reliance on internal funding will permit (Vanacker and Manigart, 2010). As the evidence presented earlier suggests, in many countries firms face significant barriers in accessing any external finance rather than having the choice between alternative financing options which pecking order models outline.

A second influence on the capital or financing structure of firms in more developed economies is sometimes said to be the 'debt-tax shield'. The basic argument here is that because the cost of servicing debt (i.e. interest payments) is automatically tax deductible, external debt can reduce tax liability, i.e. debt can act as a tax shield. For example, in the case of an established and profitable business, any interest payments on external debt financing will reduce its corporation tax liability by reducing operating profit. This may make it tax efficient for the company to carry a high debt burden. Consider, however, the case of a high-tech start-up in, say, biotechnology. Here profitability may be low or negative, and R&D expenditure high. The potential value of the debt-tax shield is reduced – as there are few if any profits to offset. In this case debt is less attractive and equity funding may be more attractive both because of its financial and its signalling benefits. It may also be that the firm's R&D spending provides an alternative tax credit (Mansfield, 1986). Like the pecking order hypothesis, discussion of the strategic implications of the debt-tax shield presupposes that firms are making a strategic choice between debt and equity financing. It also presupposes that firms are incurring a tax liability, which would not be the case for many informal enterprises in developing and transition economies. Again, therefore, discussion of the value or implications of the debt-tax shield depends crucially on aspects of the institutional environment within which a firm is located, raising questions about the value of these concepts in countries where the availability of external finance remains limited and much entrepreneurial activity remains informal.

7.3 ADDRESSING THE FINANCING GAP

Various types of supply-side measures have been implemented in different countries to try and increase the availability of capital to entrepreneurs and SMEs (Box 7.2). One of the most common types of arrangements internationally have been credit guarantee schemes (CGSs) which aim to

> encourage financial institutions, and in particular commercial banks, to lend to small businesses with viable projects and good prospects of success but which are unable to provide adequate collateral or which do not have a suitable record of financial transactions to prove that they are creditworthy.
>
> (Levitsky and Prasad, 1989, p. 2)

Internationally, very different lending objectives have been pursued by CGSs with some schemes focusing on supporting lending for working or fixed capital while others have focused on export support or development. CGSs have also proved attractive as there is some evidence that CGSs are a less costly means of expanding access to finance than directed lending. CGSs are also market friendly as the lending decision generally remains with the lending institution (Beck *et al.*, 2008b).

The central function of a CGS is that the risk of loss is shared in an agreed proportion between a lender and the guarantee organization. Ideally, the borrower is a firm with a viable project or investment but which is unable to satisfy a lender's usual lending criteria either due to a lack of collateral or an established credit rating. In this situation, and subject to some investigation of the borrower's credit-worthiness, a third party guarantee is made available to reduce the lender's exposure to risk. This insurance is likely to attract a premium over and above the lender's standard interest charges and a fee may be charged for processing or

BOX 7.2   FINANCING SMEs IN NIGERIA

In 2010 only 36.3 per cent of the Nigerian population had any engagement with the formal financial sector, the remainder relying on informal or community lending or credit services. SMEs' access to finance in Nigeria has also been limited. To increase the availability of finance to SMEs the Small and Medium Enterprises Equity Investment Scheme (SMEEIS) was introduced by Nigerian banks on a 'voluntary' basis in 2001. The scheme requires all banks in Nigeria to set aside 10 per cent of their profit after tax for either loans or equity investment in SMEs. Ten per cent of the funds set aside are allocated to micro-enterprises. As of June 2009 – the latest data available – Nigerian banks had set aside N42.02 billion ($262.81 million) under SMEEIS.

To be eligible for funding from SMEEIS firms (a) have to be registered limited companies and have to have complied with all registration requirements and (b) have to have complied with all appropriate tax laws and regulations. In addition SMEs have to meet the standard lending criteria for the banks. These strict criteria have limited the accessibility of SMEEIS funding to SMEs: 'The SMEEIS initiative has not been popular with SMEs. Even those who know about the scheme have not been able to benefit from it ... conditions for accessing SMEEIS funds were too stringent for owners of SMEs' (Isa and Terungwa, 2011, p. 407). The evidence also points to a decline in bank lending to SMEs in Nigeria since the introduction of SMEEIS with banks particularly reticent to lend to smaller, more risky, companies. This leads to the conclusion that 'SMEEIS has been unable to make any significant positive impact on the financing of SMEs in Nigeria ... the financing mix of SMEs is predominantly from informal sources of finance'. Isa and Terungwa (2011) highlight the potential importance of other forms of policy initiative including, potentially, a credit guarantee scheme.

Sources: Isa and Terungwa (2011) and http://www.cenbank.org

investigating the guarantee application. In this respect the UK's Small Firms Loan Guarantee Scheme is fairly typical (Box 7.3).

Drawing on a survey of CGSs in over 60 countries a recent World Bank survey provides a useful overview of global CGS activity (Beck *et al.*, 2008a):

■   CGSs are found to vary widely in age and size with the oldest being established in Uruguay in 1896 and with a sharp increase in the number of schemes established since 2000.

BOX 7.3 SMALL FIRMS LOAN GUARANTEE SCHEME (UK)

The UK Small Firms Loan Guarantee Scheme (SFLG) was established in 1981 to help meet the gap in the market, where small businesses with viable business proposals are unable to raise finance because of lack of security. Between June 1981 and March 2005, there were 97,000 guarantees issued with a total value of £4.2 billion ($6.9 billion). The SFLG was changed in December 2005 to focus on newer businesses. Its main features include:

■ a guarantee to the lender covering 75 per cent of the loan amount, for which the borrower pays a 2 per cent premium on the outstanding balance of the loan;

■ the ability to guarantee loans of up to £250,000 ($420,000) and with terms of up to ten years;

■ its availability to qualifying businesses with an annual turnover of up to £5.6 million ($9.3 million).

Source: UN Economic Commission for Europe (2009). *Policy Options and Instruments for Financing Innovation: A practical guide to early stage financing*, United Nations, New York and Geneva, p. 45. For further information:http://www.berr.gov.uk/bbf/enterprise-smes/info-business-owners/access-to-finance/sflg/page37607.html

■ Schemes also vary significantly in size, with mature Asian schemes (particularly the two large technology-oriented CGSs in Korea – Box 7.4) accounting for a particularly high proportion of GDP. Schemes in high-income countries are typically three times as large as those in developing economies. Penetration is greatest in Korea where outstanding loan guarantees are equivalent to over 9 per cent of GDP or almost 10 per cent of total banking credit to the private sector.

■ The vast majority (95 per cent of CGSs in the World Bank study) are restricted either in terms of their sectoral coverage, geographical focus or target clients: 24 per cent are restricted to a specific geographical area, with 45 per cent established to assist SMEs.

■ Two governance structures dominate the profile of CGSs: mutual guarantee schemes which issue collective guarantees to loans issued by 'members' or shareholders and publicly operated schemes operated at the local, regional or national level.

BOX 7.4   CGSs IN SOUTH KOREA

Two major national guarantee funds operate in Korea: KODIT or the Korea Credit Guarantee Fund was established in 1961 and provides a general guarantee facility for all types of business loans, and the Korea Technology Credit Guarantee fund – which as of September 2009 is called KOTEC – was established in 1989 and focuses on guarantee facilities for projects involving an element of new technology. Both funds are substantial in size and national in coverage and KODIT is part-funded by a national levy on loans made by the banking industry (currently 0.15 per cent). Both are also established as independent not-for-profit institutions and operate a loan-level approvals system for guarantees.

KODIT provides guarantees for working capital and a range of other bank loans. In 2008 total outstanding loan guarantees were 30.387 billion Korean wan (around $26 billion) of which 84 per cent were guarantees for bank loans. KODIT works by requiring firms seeking loan guarantees to submit an application either electronically or in person. A process of consultation and investigation then contributes to the evaluation of the guarantee application. If the guarantee is approved the firm is issued with a Letter of Credit Guarantee for which the firm pays a guarantee fee (0.5 per cent to 3.0 per cent APR of the outstanding guarantee). The extent of the guarantee will depend on the credit rating of the firm and will vary from 50 to 85 per cent of the value of the loan.

KOTEC was founded in 1989 to provide credit guarantees to facilitate financing for new technology-based enterprises while promoting the growth of technologically strong small and medium enterprises (SMEs) and venture businesses. Since its foundation, KOTEC has provided a total of US$99.7 billion (₩104.1 trillion) in guarantees. A key element of KOTEC's guarantee procedure is technology appraisal which is undertaken by a national network of Technology Appraisal Centres (TACs). Potential bank borrowers who cannot meet a bank's lending criteria – which usually means the borrower cannot provide satisfactory collateral – are referred by banks to the TACs. KOTEC staff then carry out an independent appraisal of the loan guarantee application investigating both commercial and technological aspects of the application. If the case is suitable for a guarantee, the borrower is provided with a Letter of Guarantee which is taken to the bank. As with KODIT the guarantee involves the payment of a guarantee fee, the amount depending on the size of the amount being guaranteed.

Kang and Heshmati (2008) considered the effects of the Korean credit and technology credit guarantee schemes on the survival and performance of SMEs over the 2001 to 2004 period. Their analysis of over 200,702 applications for credit from KODIT and KOTEC concluded that:

■ Credit guarantee agencies were more likely to provide guarantees to firms which are less risky and to provide larger guarantees to larger firms and those with more collateral.

■ Credit guarantees had a generally positive effect on performance, promoting growth in sales and productivity but having a less clear effect on employment stability.

■ Firms whose loans were guaranteed by KOTEC had a higher survival probability than those guaranteed by KODIT. 'One of the reasons in the difference between two groups stems from the technology evaluation process ... In this respect, KOTEC provided some part of guarantee for new technology-based firms by evaluating technology, and so helped mitigate credit rationing partially' (Kang and Heshmati, 2008, p. 453).

Sources: http://eng.kodit.co.kr and http://www.kotec.or.kr

■ The predominant form of guarantee provided by CGSs is a direct loan guarantee with 72 per cent of schemes operating a 'loan-level' assessment (involving both an eligibility check and a risk profile). A smaller proportion of schemes (23 per cent) adopt a portfolio screening approach in which approved lenders manage risk within a portfolio of guarantees without prior approval at loan level.

CGSs have been used primarily to support the availability of loan finance to SMEs. There are, however, some examples of the use of guarantees to support equity inestment (Aernoudt et al., 2007), although there is little consensus about the effectiveness of these schemes (Wright et al., 2006). Other supply-side measures have focused on 'equity gaps' and trying to ensure adequate equity financing for SMEs at different stages of development. Here, there is a need to recognize the potential value of both informal and formal private equity funding and that facilitating investment by business angels may require specific legislative frameworks (Robinson and Cotterell, 2007). More generally, initiatives to stimulate the development of formal venture capital markets are well known, such as the Israeli experience with the Yozma fund (Avnimelech et al., 2007). Measures to support equity investment can also involve policy intervention on the demand side. In particular, measures can be taken to strengthen firms' investment readiness, with a potential role for banks and agencies in helping businesses to assess and develop their business plans and propositions.

7.4 ISLAMIC FINANCE

Islamic finance, based on Sharia principles, has grown rapidly in recent years and provides an alternative model to conventional financing principles. The first fully fledged Islamic Bank, Dubai Islamic Bank, was founded in 1975 and since then Islamic finance has grown rapidly with 456 institutions in 54 countries providing Islamic finance products in 2010. The 'Top 500 Islamic Financial Institutions' produced by *The Banker* magazine suggested that Sharia compliant assets rose by 8.85 per cent from $822 billion in 2009 to $895 billion in 2010, with Islamic finance achieving a compound annual growth rate of 23.46 per cent from 2006 to 2010 (http://top500islamic.thebanker.com). As Visser (2009) notes, however, this remains small compared to the value of conventionally held assets. UBS alone for example had invested assets of $638 billion in 2011 (http://www.ubs.com). At the country level, Iran, Saudi Arabia and Malaysia were the world's leaders in Islamic finance assets in 2009 (Table 7.4).

The key principle which governs Islamic finance is the prohibition of interest payments or the

> prohibition of *riba,* any predetermined or fixed return in financial transactions. As stated in the Quran: 'Allah forbids riba and permits trade.' While there is much debate about the exact nature of this prohibition on riba, there exists a widespread perception that the ban on riba implies a ban on interest.
>
> (Aggarwal and Yousef, 2000, p. 96)

Instead, it is suggested, a provider of capital should share the business risks – both upside and downside – with an entrepreneur. This principle is called profit-and-

Table 7.4 *Top 10 countries with Sharia compliant assets in 2009*

		Sharia compliant assets ($bm)
1	Iran	314,897
2	Saudi Arabia	138,238
3	Malaysia	102,639
4	UAE	85,622
5	Kuwait	69,088
6	Bahrain	44,858
7	Qatar	34,676
8	Turkey	22,561
9	UK	18,949
10	Bangladesh	9,259

Source: Abou-Gabal et al. (2011).

loss sharing (PLS). In some contexts this can simply look like a conventional equity investment in which business gains and losses are shared in proportion to the investor's equity stake. In other situations, lenders may bear the whole cost of any failure. Visser (2009) identifies two types of PLS financial instruments: mudaraba (or qirad) and musharaka. In mudaraba or trustee financing the bank provides the entire capital needs of a project and then essentially acts as a sleeping partner with profit shares being agreed in advance. The mudarib (entrepreneur) then develops the project. If things go well profits are shared in line with the initial agreement; if the project fails the bank bears all of the losses. Musharaka, or partnership financing, looks more like a conventional equity investment or joint venture agreement with profits and losses, generally, shared in line with the investor's equity stake. As Visser (2009) highlights, both types of PLS contracts involve agency issues, a misalignment of rewards and capital risks, which are particularly important in mudaraba. These agency issues are exacerbated in musharaka as Islamic law does not allow collateral in this type of financing arrangement and the bank also has no right to monitor the investment or participate in the project. As a result most major Islamic banks allocate only a small proportion of funding to PLS financial instruments. In 2006, for example, Dubai Islamic Bank had 25.3 per cent of its portfolio in PLS instruments and 74.7 in other types of assets (Abou-Gabal *et al.*, 2011).

Other Islamic financial instruments such as murabaha are based on the notion of a mark-up or cost-plus arrangement and are more akin to conventional debt financing. Used generally as a means of trade finance or working capital this involves the bank purchasing goods which it sells to the entrepreneur including a mark-up. The entrepreneur then resells the goods and repays the loan. Here again, agency problems arise as the bank is the original purchaser of the goods and is dependent on the entrepreneur to complete the deal. Murabaha can also involve more significant transaction costs as it requires a financier to develop two contracts: one with the seller of the goods and one with the entrepreneur. Another form of mark-up or cost-plus instrument is ijara which is akin to a conventional leasing arrangement. Here, a bank purchases an asset and allows an entrepreneur to use it for a set fee. Ownership of the asset remains with the bank, although an agreement may be made to sell the asset to the entrepreneur after some period of use (Aggarwal and Yousef, 2000). Debates continue about whether financing arrangements based on a mark-up are Halal (Aggarwal and Yousef, 2000, Visser, 2009). More broadly, however, it has been argued that adherence to the principles of Islamic financing – an emphasis on PLS – would increase the amount of capital available to entrepreneurs, ensure more equitable distribution of income and improve the efficiency of capital allocation (Banks, 1995).

Abou-Gabal *et al.* (2011) consider the challenges for Islamic finance institutions in supporting entrepreneurship noting that like conventional banks Islamic banks face disproportionately high transaction costs and risk in dealing with entrepreneurs

BOX 7.5 MURABAHA MICRO-FINANCE IN INDONESIA

The development of Islamic finance in Indonesia has been spectacular in recent years. Particularly rapid growth has been seen in Islamic micro-finance institutions or BMTs. BMTs are Islamic micro-finance institutions, established by individuals or groups to help micro-entrepreneurs as a strategy for eradicating rural poverty, especially in villages or traditional markets. By 2006, more than 3,000 BMTs had been established.

BMT Al-Ikhlas was established in 1995 in Yogyakarta and declared itself to be operated on cooperative and Sharia principles in 1997. Al-Ikhlas provides a range of Shariah compliant savings and financing products including timed deposit accounts, PLS and Ijarah financing. To be eligible for murabaha funding customers must: be a member of the BMT; fill out an application form provided by BMT management completely and honestly; have a good personality; be responsible and trustworthy; be aged 18–60 years; and be prepared to comply with due diligence investigation by BMT staff. Al-Ikhlas may also require an 'authorization letter of taking over a collateral good guaranteed to the BMT' (p. 175). After any due diligence is carried out the profit margin of the murabaha is determined in negotiation between the client and the BMT. The operation of the murabaha depends on the type of goods involved. Where transactions are simple (e.g. television, air conditioner, motorcycle) the BMT will undertake the purchase and send the goods to the customer's address. Where the murabaha is for goods for further sale (e.g. petrol, vegetables) the BMT will provide cash to the applicant and allow them to purchase the goods directly. The minimum profit rate in a murabaha contract at BMTs is 24–30 per cent of total financing. Compared with the interest rate in conventional banking at 17–20 per cent per year, the profit rates with BMT financing are higher.

Source: Kholis (2008)

but face the added difficulty that in some situations collateral-based lending is not an option. This often makes it difficult for Islamic finance institutions to support entrepreneurs although there are interesting examples of the application of Islamic finance principles to micro-finance and community-based lending in a number of countries (Obaidullah and Latiff, 2008). In Malaysia, for example, there are now over 3,000 community-based Islamic finance micro-finance organizations (see Box 7.5).

7.5 SUMMARY AND KEY POINTS

Finance is a perennial issue for the vast majority of businesses with the lack of suitable finance and its cost among the most common concerns. International evidence suggests that small firms are less likely to use external finance than larger firms and may be more seriously impacted by weaknesses in capital supplies (Beck *et al.*, 2008a). Bruton *et al.* (2009), for example, examine the development of the venture capital industry in the rapidly developing economies of Latin America and Asia and conclude ' . . . institutions cannot only limit behaviour, they can also enable actions by actors as they seek to navigate their environment' (p. 775). Measures to increase capital availability have therefore been seen as almost universally important with countries often implementing measures either to directly increase capital supplies to SMEs or reduce the risks of SME lending through credit guarantee schemes. The lack of availability of external finance – particularly equity finance – in many countries also emphasizes the limited relevance of standard conceptual models such as the pecking order hypothesis. Basic distinctions between internal and external finance and debt and equity funding remain relevant wherever firms do have alternative funding sources.

7.6 DISCUSSION QUESTIONS AND FURTHER READING

Both supply and demand factors seem important in terms of enabling small firms and entrepreneurs to access appropriate finance. On the demand side see in particular Kon and Storey (2003). On the supply side see Beck *et al.* (2008a) for an international perspective and Avnimelech *et al.* (2007) for a more in-depth, national, perspective on the relationship between capital market supply-side initiatives and other types of support for high-tech firms.

The material reviewed in this chapter suggests the following discussion questions:

1   What does the evidence suggest? Is the main issue with the availability of business finance on the demand side or the supply side? Does this differ between developed and developing economies?
2   In the financing of Footfall (Box 7.1) what was the most important type of financing? Think about which type of finance was most crucial for the survival of the firm.
3   Supply-side supports take various forms. What could have been done to ensure the SMEEIS measure in Nigeria was more successful as a means of providing finance for smaller firms?

Chapter 8

Small firms and innovation

8.1 INTRODUCTION

Entrepreneurs and small firms have an almost mythological place in thinking about innovation. In Silicon Valley, small firms are associated with the inventiveness and creativity associated with the computer and IT sector (Saxenian, 1996), while in Cambridge, UK, small university spin-out companies have helped drive biotechnology and regional development (Druilhe and Garnsey, 2003). Other studies have emphasized the role of small firms in commercializing new research results and opening up new markets (Roberts, 1991, Lockett *et al.*, 2003). In this chapter we explore the role of small firms in innovation. Key themes are: the heterogeneity of small companies – and therefore, the difficulty of generalization; the specific barriers which entrepreneurs and small firms face in undertaking innovation and the managerial and strategic challenges these pose. The key learning objectives therefore are:

- To introduce the notion of innovation and its conceptual and empirical relationship to entrepreneurship.
- To explore the strengths and weaknesses of small firms in terms of their ability to innovate and how these might vary across different national and international contexts.
- To evaluate a range of different policy instruments which have been used to overcome the barriers to innovation by entrepreneurs and small firms.

First, however, it is useful to be clear about what we mean by the term 'innovation'. Although definitions vary they generally stress the commercialization of new knowledge or technology to generate increased sales or business value. The US Advisory Committee on Measuring Innovation, for example, defines innovation as: 'The design, invention, development and/or implementation of new or altered products, services, processes, systems, organizational structures or business models for the purpose of creating new value for customers and financial returns for the firm' (Advisory Committee on Measuring Innovation in the 21st Century Economy, 2008, p. i). Or, in more concrete terms, innovations can be thought of as new, or perhaps improved, products or services which are created from diverse knowledge inputs (Hansen and Birkinshaw, 2007). The key point here is the commercialization aspect, or as Von Stamm (2003) puts it, innovation = creativity + commercialization.

Innovations vary of course in terms of their focus – i.e. product, service, organization or business model – and their degree of novelty (see Boxes 8.1 and 8.2). Olson *et al.* (1995) suggest a four-way classification of product innovations reflecting this latter aspect identifying:

- **new to the world products** – which are new to the market and to the company introducing them;
- **line extensions** – which are new to the marketplace but not the company;
- **me-too products** – which are new to the company but not the marketplace; and
- **product or service modifications** – which are neither new to the company or the marketplace but simply an upgrade of existing market offerings.

But why should firms invest in innovation? Baumol (2002) argues that in free market economies innovation is a necessity if a firm wants to survive. Other evidence suggests that innovating firms outperform non-innovators in a number of ways. First, the evidence suggests that innovators are more profitable than non-innovators (Geroski *et al.*, 1993, Leiponen, 2000). Second, innovating firms also tend to grow faster and have higher productivity than non-innovating firms (Cainelli *et al.*, 2004, Crepon *et al.*, 1998, Loof and Heshmati, 2001, 2002). Cainelli *et al.* (2006), for example, examine the interaction between innovation and performance and conclude that there is a two-way relationship: innovative firms outperform non-innovators, but better performing firms are also more likely to innovate and to devote more of their resources to innovation. They conclude that there is 'a cumulative, a self-reinforcing mechanism' linking innovation and performance (p. 454). Similar evidence that the impact of innovation is contingent on other activities emerges from the literature on innovation and exporting. There is evidence of a positive link between innovation and exporting (Wakelin, 1998, Sterlacchini, 1999, Bleaney and Wakelin, 2002, Roper and Love, 2002, Lachenmaier and Wobmann, 2006) but also evidence of a positive relationship between exporting and innovation (Blind and Jumgmittag, 2004, Love *et al.*, 2010). A recent review by Rosenbusch *et al.* (2011) also suggests that the effects of innovation on SME performance may also depend both on the cultural context and the age of the firm.

Given evidence of such positive effects, it is not surprising that developing innovative products or services is a high priority for many firms, something that

BOX 8.1 'SHARPER SOLUTIONS' – BERNHARD AND COMPANY LTD

Based in Rugby, UK, Bernhard and Company Ltd was established in 1984 and specializes in developing and manufacturing spin grinding machines for sharpening grass mower blades. Spin grinding of mower blades enables a very accurate, hollow ground blade edge to be produced allowing considerable time-saving over traditional back-lapping and relief grinding. The firm has around 30 employees and its spin grinding products are used by over three-quarters of the US top 100 golf courses and leading golf clubs and sports turf facilities worldwide. In 2008 the company was awarded a Queen's Award for Enterprise: Innovation based on the continuous innovation and development of the Express Dual and Anglemaster sharpening systems. The company is headed by its founder and principal shareholder Stephen Bernhard who, in the past, has also taken a lead role in shaping the firm's R&D agenda. One member of staff involved in R&D commented:

> Stephen for example has always been the person who has driven R&D. He would come up with things that are issues in the field. Also you get the customer who will approach you with an idea or a problem and you make a note of it. My personal feedback tends to be when I get to visit a customer like I did yesterday or if I go to the national show in the US I ask questions to try to identify valuable ideas . . . I would be happy to receive more from the sales guys.

The basic technology for the spin or rotary grinding machines was originally developed by Atterton & Ellis Ltd, which was established in 1941 and was subsequently acquired and improved by Bernhard and Co.

Sources: http://www.bernhard.co.uk; and unpublished MA Dissertation by Friede, G. R. (2006) 'Social capital and relational embeddedness in intra and interfirm networks: A managerial perspective', available at: http://edissertations.nottingham.ac.uk/519/1/06malixgf.pdf

BOX 8.2   WOMEN LIKE US CIC

London-based recruitment consultancy and social enterprise 'Women Like Us' provides an innovative service to help women with children get back to work and employers find experienced part-time workers. Co-founders Karen Mattison and Emma Stewart, both mothers, were working as business consultants when they realized there was a gap in the recruitment market to help mothers with children find flexible work. Karen Mattison is quoted as saying: 'Employers were telling us that they were struggling to recruit good, experienced part-time workers, while mums at the school gates were telling us that they really wanted to get back to work but didn't know where to go.'

The company provides: career coaching, guidance for women on their journey back to work, a recruitment service to help women find part-time jobs, a job design service and an executive search service for employers interested in providing flexible working. For example, one of the clients of Women Like Us was Energy Design Studio, which was looking for a high-level marketing professional who wanted to mix a senior role with flexible hours.

'I had been looking for someone for months, and though good candidates had been coming through, they had all been looking for full-time work which would have been too much for us,' said Andrew Rose of Energy Design Studio. 'We got in touch and the candidates they put forward were all women who had built up impressive careers in marketing and were now looking to pick those careers up again in a part-time role to fit around their families. . . . We interviewed, chose our new marketer and now a month in, it is going very well'.

Women Like Us changed its legal status to become a Community Interest Company (CIC) in 2007. CICs are limited companies with a social objective, with any profits from the business being reinvested. Karen Mattison commented that:

> By operating as a CIC, Women Like Us is able to protect its social mission, giving assurance to our school partners, government funders and other key stakeholders that we are achieving our social aim . . . at the same time, it also allows us to operate as a business, working with employers and government on commercial terms.

Sources: http://www.womenlikeus.org.uk and
http://www.bis.gov.uk/cicregulator

requires both investment and organization. Baumol (2002, p. ix), for example, comments that:

> . . . firms cannot afford to leave innovation to chance. Rather, managements are forced by market pressures to support innovation activity systematically . . . The result is a ferocious arms race among firms in the most rapidly evolving sectors of the economy, with innovation as the prime weapon.

For start-up companies and SMEs which lack the technical and financial resources of larger firms, innovation poses particular challenges (Vossen, 1998).

8.2 INNOVATION AND ENTREPRENEURSHIP – TWO SIDES OF THE SAME COIN?

Historically, thinking about innovation and entrepreneurship have gone very much hand-in-hand. Both are, after all, the process of creating value from knowledge assets. This duality has been summarized as follows: '[Innovation] . . . is the specific function of entrepreneurship . . . [it] is the means by which the entrepreneur either creates new wealth producing resources or endows existing resources with enhanced potential for creating wealth' (Drucker, 1993). Drucker's comment is consistent with what has come to be known as the Schumpeter Mark 1 model which was discussed in Chapter 3.

One conceptual approach to understanding SME innovation – used for example by Robson *et al*. (2009) in their recent study of innovation in Ghana – is resource dependency theory. This emphasizes the dependency of entrepreneurs and small firms on the institutional and organizational environment within which entrepreneurs and small firms are situated and the potential impacts on firms' innovation activity. In particular, Robson *et al*. (2009) argue that small firms located in urban centres in Ghana will have greater opportunities for networking than those in more rural areas, with potentially positive impacts on innovation outcomes. In the spirit of the Schumpeter Mark 1 model, other researchers have also emphasized the importance of the institutional context in which innovative entrepreneurs operate, focusing on the role of entrepreneurs in exploiting otherwise unexploited knowledge. Audretsch (2005), for example, proposes a 'knowledge spillovers theory of entrepreneurship' in which development is led by innovative start-up businesses based on otherwise unexploited knowledge, i.e. that 'the creation of a new firm is the endogenous response to investments in knowledge that have not been entirely or exhaustively appropriated by the incumbent firms' (Audretsch, 2007, p. 95). Empirical evidence suggests that the potential for such innovative start-ups is greatest where investments in new knowledge are high and there are significant levels of entrepreneurial capital, i.e.

BOX 8.3 BUCKING THE TREND IN MEXICO – THE BIOCLON INSTITUTE

Mexico has a particular problem with people – particularly children – being stung or bitten by poisonous animals. The Bioclon Institute is a research-focused Mexican SME which aims to make use of new biotech developments to become a worldwide leader in the R&D of antivenins. The firm was established in 1990 as a merger of biological and pharmaceutical companies. The company has around 7 per cent of the global market of antivenins and sales have doubled over the last four years. The strategy of the business has recognized that the innovation system of Mexico is not strong and therefore success for the firm depends strongly on its own internal resources, i.e. its 'capability for developing, adopting, and incorporating state-of-the-art products, equipment, process, operation and organizational technologies'. This led to the development of a technology management model incorporating links to leading edge institutions, connections to a customer community and internal IP management and development strategies. According to Bioclon Institute President Lic. Juan López de Silanes:

> the competitive advantages have been a result of efforts developed under a strategic plan based on continual innovation of processes and products, using a model of technology management supported by a strong academic-industrial connections program that seeks to promote modernization and impel research on a national level through grants and stimuli for researchers, development of providers, and improvement in manufacturing processes.

Sources: Solleiro *et al.* (2006) and http://www.bioclon.com.mx

'the milieu of agents and institutions that are conducive to the creation of new firms' (Audretsch 2005, p. 49). Stuart and Sorenson (2003), for example, emphasize the role of local resources – university connections, venture capital and skills – for the birth of new Canadian biotechnology firms. Some firms are however, capable of bucking the trend in this respect. (Box 8.3).

8.3 SMALL FIRMS IN THE INNOVATION LANDSCAPE

Unlike levels of entrepreneurial activity there are few truly global indicators of innovative activity. International comparisons of research and development spending are possible, but these reflect an input into the innovation process rather than an indication of outputs, and are also relevant only for more technological innovation. Patent comparisons can also be used, although these again suffer from the limitation of being an indication of inventive rather than innovative output – i.e. without the commercialization phase (OECD, 2008a). Usai (2011), for example, examines the distribution of inventive activity across OECD countries and regions using internationally registered patents per million population as the key indicator. So which are the most inventive countries? A group of European economies top the inventiveness league table: Switzerland, Finland, Sweden and Denmark (Table 8.1). More broadly, however, a range of Southern and Eastern European economies perform less well, meaning that Asia (dominated by Japan and Korea) emerges as the most innovative macro-area, followed by North America (Figure 8.1).

As the regional analysis conducted by Usai (2011) suggests there are also significant within-country differences in inventiveness with some of the largest variations occurring in the Netherlands, USA, Germany and Switzerland. By and large, higher levels of inventiveness are associated with larger population centres and major cities suggesting the generality of the positive link between an urban location and innovation identified by Robson *et al.* (2009) in Ghana. Usai (2011) also notes, however, that across the OECD a dispersion of inventiveness is taking place with urban centres losing some of their historical dominance of invention.

Table 8.1 *Inventive performance by country – OECD countries, 2002–4*

	Patents per million population	Rank		Patents per million population	Rank
Switzerland	233.00	1	Canada	73.60	16
Finland	228.30	2	Luxembourg	70.40	17
Sweden	204.90	3	Korea	69.10	18
Denmark	184.00	4	United Kingdom	67.40	19
Germany	172.50	5	Ireland	66.30	20
Netherlands	160.10	6	Italy	34.70	21
Iceland	142.20	7	Spain	16.80	22
United States	141.20	8	Hungary	15.10	23
Japan	129.50	9	Czech Republic	7.00	24
Austria	106.20	10	Slovak Republic	5.30	25
Norway	98.20	11	Greece	3.70	26
Australia	94.20	12	Poland	2.00	27
New Zealand	84.90	13	Turkey	1.90	28
France	82.00	14	Portugal	1.60	29
Belgium	74.90	15	Mexico	1.30	30

Source: Usai (2011), Table 1.

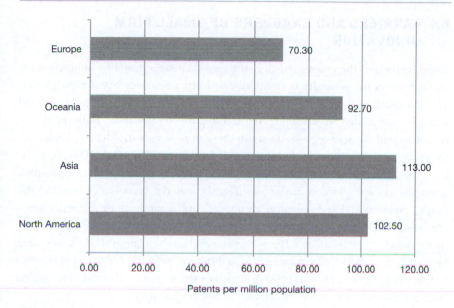

Figure 8.1
Inventive performance by region – OECD countries

Source: Usai (2011), Table 2.

No international data is collected on patents by smaller and larger firms but information is available from surveys on the innovation activity of different sizes of firms. This provides a sense of the level of innovative activity among smaller firms compared to larger firms. Table 8.2, for example, gives data for the proportion of firms in Ireland introducing new or improved products for six three-year periods since the early 1990s. What is clear here is that the proportion of innovating firms increases with firm size in each period although there is also some variation from period to period. We examine the reasons why this might be the case in the next section.

Table 8.2 *Proportion of Irish firms introducing product innovations – by size*

	1991–1993	1994–1996	1997–1999	2000–2002	2003–2005	2006–2008
	% Firms	% Firms	% Firms	% Firms	% Firms	% Firms
10–20 employees	40.6	50.0	57.3	41.1	57.7	54.1
20–49 employees	62.3	64.8	58.2	53.7	73.6	69.5
50 plus employees	75.8	76.0	76.1	76.7	77.1	76.1

Source: Irish Innovation Pannel, author's analysis.

8.4 BARRIERS AND ENABLERS OF SMALL FIRM INNOVATION

Consideration of the managerial and strategic challenges posed by innovation for entrepreneurs has generally been addressed from a resource-based view (RBV). This emphasizes that firms comprise heterogeneous bundles of tangible and intangible assets that are valuable, rare and imperfectly imitable. 'Both the skills/ resources and the way organizations use them must constantly change, leading to the creation of continuously changing temporary advantages' (Fiol, 2001, p. 692). In terms of innovation this leads Vossen (1998, p. 90) to conclude that 'the relative strengths of large business are predominantly material (economies of scale and scope, financial and technological resources, etc.), while those of small firms are mostly behavioral (entrepreneurial dynamism, flexibility, efficiency, proximity to the market, motivation)'. Recent evidence based on innovation survey data highlights the relative importance of these different factors in constraining innovation activity. Hewitt-Dundas (2006) identifies three groups of constraints which have consistently been shown to reduce innovation activity:

- financial constraints – lack of finance and low rate of return;
- human resource constraints – risk of development, employee attitudes, lack of market opportunities, lack of info about new technologies, lack of technical expertise, lack of managerial expertise;
- organizational constraints – regulatory requirements and lack of partners.

The impact of each constraint is then tested on the innovation activities of a large sample of Irish firms. The key findings being that the profile of resource constraints that impact on innovation are broadly similar in larger and smaller firms although a lack of finance, limited market opportunities and legislative or regulatory issues are more often important in smaller firms. It is concluded that:

> This supports other research suggesting that advantages (disadvantages) of large plants are mainly material (behavioral) while the advantages (disadvantages) of small plants are behavioral (material) . . . For small plants the most important barrier to undertaking product innovation is a lack of external partners. In contrast, for larger plants it is the high risk of development or a lack of internal expertise which present the greatest barrier to product innovation.
>
> (Hewitt-Dundas, 2006, p. 273)

These results suggest the balance of strategic and managerial issues which innovation leaders face in small and large companies. In larger firms, issues are likely to relate to perceived risk, establishing investment priorities, human resources, and ensuring effective and timely resource allocation. While, in smaller firms, issues relate more to project selection, resource acquisition and the identification of potential development partners. These differences lead to very different managerial approaches to innovation in larger and smaller firms, although these reflect broader differences in management in these firms. In larger firms, innovation – new product, service or process development – tends to be a more formally organized activity, a specialist function, with well-developed project management practices. In small firms, by contrast, innovation is very often an ad hoc activity driven by opportunity or interest rather than strategy, and undertaken informally alongside firms' other activities.

One other area in which important strategic differences emerge between small and larger firms is in their approach to intellectual property (IP) management and protection. In some industries – notably biotechnology – firms of all sizes have similar propensities to patent; in other sectors, however, smaller firms may find it difficult to defend patents legally and therefore may be more reluctant to invest in IP protection (Blackburn, 2003). Lanjouw and Schankerman (2004) provide some insight into the issue of whether small firms are able to defend their IP. Aside from resource considerations Lanjouw and Schankerman (2004) argue there are two other reasons why small firms might find it difficult to defend patent rights and so might be less likely to invest in R&D:

- Small firms tend to have few patents and are, therefore, less able to adopt a technology swapping mechanism to defend their IP rights than larger companies which may have a wider patent portfolio.
- Smaller firms may also have fewer repeated interactions with the other party in any dispute – a liability of newness type argument – and so, there are fewer incentives to solve any issue cooperatively.

Lanjouw and Schankerman (2004) match data from the United States Patent and Trademark Office (USPTO) and courts and identify the proportion of patents which ended up in dispute. Key findings suggest that the majority of cases are settled before getting to court but that small firms are – as predicted – more likely to be involved in court proceedings than larger firms although the evidence on outcomes is less clear. In general, they argue that it is more difficult for small firms to defend IP than larger companies who may have more strategic options in terms of avoiding costly court proceedings.

8.5 SUMMARY AND KEY POINTS

Innovation and entrepreneurship are often equated in the research literature although the two activities are rather different. Both have in common the commercialization of knowledge, but innovation focuses on the introduction of a new product, process, service or business model often in an existing organization, while entrepreneurship typically focuses more specifically on the creation of a new organization. Notions of intrapreneurship – entrepreneurship from within an existing organization – seek to bridge this gap.

Resource-based theoretical perspectives and empirical studies such as Hewitt-Dundas (2006) emphasize the resource disadvantages of smaller firms

BOX 8.4 SUPPORTING SME INNOVATION

Policy support for innovation in SMEs has been an active area of development in recent years. For example, most countries provide some forms of tax breaks or tax credits for R&D and innovation spending, although take-up of these among smaller firms is often limited. Many countries also provide grant support for innovation in smaller firms often with a focus on technologically based innovation and on those firms located in more peripheral or under-developed regions. Less common is support for service sector or non-technological innovation although there are some good examples of schemes such as the SERVE scheme operated by the Finnish government agency TEKES. This aims to encourage the development of innovative service concepts and service business models with a particular focus on SMEs. Other support measures focus on addressing small firms' difficulty in identifying and forming relationships with other innovation partners (Hewitt-Dundas, 2006). Innovation Voucher schemes, for example, have been implemented in a number of countries with the objective of stimulating new innovative partnerships.

EU policy has also focused on promoting innovation in small firms as part of the wider Lisbon Agenda, designed to close the competitiveness gap between Europe and the US. EU programmes have been implemented both to encourage SMEs to undertake collaborative R&D and to help improve innovation capability. For example the Competitiveness and Innovation Framework Programme (CIP) provides EU funding to support innovation and development by promoting technological entrepreneurship, ICT development and energy efficiency. This is supported by other initiatives such as IMP[3]rove which aims to encourage SMEs to develop and improve their innovation management capabilities. Comprising an online assessment and subsequent consultancy support, IMP[3]rove offers SMEs a chance to improve their innovation management performance.

Source: EU policy, available at:
http://europa.eu/scadplus/glossary/lisbon_strategy_en.htm

in innovation. These are offset to some extent by behavioural advantages linked to flexibility etc. However, in most countries smaller firms remain less innovation prone than larger firms and this is often seen as a case for policy intervention. Policy interventions differ markedly between countries but in general they seek to reduce the risks or costs of innovation for smaller firms or overcome barriers to networking or alliance formation (Box 8.4).

8.6 DISCUSSION QUESTIONS AND FURTHER READING

Vossen (1998) provides a baseline account of the strengths and weaknesses of small firms for innovation. A more recent empirical analysis can be found in Hewitt-Dundas (2006). For those interested in the geography of innovative activity, Usai (2011) provides a comprehensive account, while Blackburn (2003) focuses on the use of IP protection by smaller firms in the UK.

The issues outlined here suggest the following discussion questions:

1. How would you describe the innovations undertaken by Bernhard and Company (Box 8.1) and Women Like Us (Box 8.2)? Radical or incremental? Does it matter?
2. What institutional conditions are necessary for entrepreneurship to contribute to innovation? Is this something that happens everywhere?
3. What determines whether innovation in a particular sector is dominated by smaller or larger firms?

Chapter 9

Antisocial, unlawful and criminal enterprise

9.1 INTRODUCTION

In previous chapters we have focused on for-profit entrepreneurship but another area of life in which we find some highly 'entrepreneurial' activity is organized crime or antisocial enterprise. From Somali pirates to the activities of the Mafia or the Yakuza, organized crime has become a feature of every world economy and has been estimated to be a $2 trillion industry worldwide, roughly the equivalent of the annual GDP of the UK, or twice global defence spending. Of this the World Federation of United Nations Associations estimated in 2007 that the largest sector, estimated at around $520 billion, is counterfeit or pirated goods; drug trading accounts for an estimated $320 billion with human trafficking a further $44 billion (Borger, 2007).

At the local level, criminal enterprise comes down to individuals. Pearson and Hobbs (2003), for example, describe the drug-dealing activities of 'Alf' and his boss 'Frank Robins' (Box 9.1). The middle-market drug-dealing activities of Alf and Frank display many of the characteristics which we might normally associate with entrepreneurship: opportunity recognition, risk-taking, the development of an effective team and the importance of networks. But can, or should, we call their criminal activities entrepreneurial? Or, put another way, does entrepreneurship have a moral dimension? We consider this question in Section 9.2, highlighting the extent to which notions of entrepreneurship – and *inter alia* some aspects of morality – can be viewed as socially situated or socially constructed (Anderson and Smith, 2007).

A second issue raised by the case study of Frank Robins and Alf (Box 9.1), however, is why they chose to become involved in criminal enterprise rather than some more legitimate form of activity. Section 9.3 focuses on this question, drawing on Becker's (1968) notion of rational crime and Smith's (1980) notion of a spectrum of enterprise. Both suggest the possibility that for some people in some situations a life of crime may be a 'rational' choice. They also emphasize

BOX 9.1   MIDDLE-MARKET DRUG DEALING

Pearson and Hobbs (2003) report a case study of the 'middle-market' or wholesale drug-dealing activities of Frank Robins, the boss, and Alf his runner. Based in Northern England the case describes how Robins and Alf had achieved a dominant position in their local market, buying and selling large quantities of drugs and linking into various other individuals and networks.

Both Alf and Frank had grown up in the town in which their drug-dealing activities took place and had played football on the same team when they were kids. Alf had started working for Frank when he was unemployed and when Frank's previous runner had been arrested losing £150,000 ($240,000) of Frank's money in the process. Alf and Frank were therefore very aware of the risks they were taking. Frank's family was also involved in the business: Alf used to pick up drugs from Frank's father's house while Frank's auntie used her kitchen equipment to dilute heroin to help maximize profits.

In addition to Frank Robins, there was another local drug dealer named Colin Percy. Both Robins and Percy were running profitable businesses and often found cooperation to be more congenial than conflict. When either ran short of particular drugs, for example, they would often supply each other.

again the value of a neo-institutionalist, contextualized perspective on entrepreneurship which recognizes the importance of the institutional context in which choices are made but also acknowledges the agency of individuals. Section 9.4 develops this argument a little further adopting the process perspective developed by Albanese (2000) to provide a link between an individual's local environment and opportunities, their skill set and career choices.

By the end of this chapter – and after considering the discussion questions outlined in Section 9.5 – students will be:

- familiar with debates about the moral status of entrepreneurship, the notion that entrepreneurship is a socially constructed concept and the difficulties of applying moral and legal yardsticks;
- able to apply an institutionalist approach to criminal enterprise including an understanding of the role of structure and agency;
- aware of the type of factors which lead individuals to make choices around antisocial enterprise.

9.2 ENTREPRENEURSHIP – THE MORAL DIMENSION

The drug-dealing activities of Frank Robins and Alf described in Pearson and Hobbs (2003) and Box 9.1 have many commonalities with the normal behaviour of entrepreneurs and those who work in small firms. Anderson and Smith (2007), however, question whether a drug-dealing business such as that operated by Frank and Alf can really be considered as 'entrepreneurship'. In particular, they focus on the morality of entrepreneurship defining morals as the 'personal values and behaviours of individuals'. Can an antisocial enterprise such as drug dealing ever be considered 'entrepreneurial'? Or, for some activity to be given the accolade 'entrepreneurship' does it need to meet a higher moral or ethical standard? Anderson and Smith (2007), for example, focus in particular on the social construction of the notion of entrepreneurship, and argue that in neoliberal societies at least the notion of the entrepreneur is heroic (Mitton, 1989). In other words, the entrepreneur is lauded as a creator of social and economic value, and the label 'entrepreneur' itself is used as a halo word (Curran, 1986) with almost religious overtones in some situations (Sorensen, 2008). This positive social construction of entrepreneurship is reinforced by media images of entrepreneurs etc. which tend to have implicit positive judgements of the social and economic value of enterprise (Nicholson and Anderson, 2005, Radu and Redien-Collot, 2008).

Anderson and Smith (2007) examine the way in which the social construction of entrepreneurship occurs through two contrasting case studies: those of 'Bill' and 'Dave'. Bill is a conventional or 'moral' entrepreneur who achieved business success through hard work and has acted as a business angel, helping others to start businesses by providing finance. Dave is a 'self-proclaimed professional criminal . . . drawn towards, and socialized into, a life of crime by the attraction of the lifestyle and by an exposure to the role models of old school villains' (Anderson and Smith, 2007, p. 490). Both Bill and Dave applied business principles to their activities (motor garages and illegal drinking clubs respectively) with Dave arguing that crime is a business which shares similar working practices to mainstream business activities. When Anderson and Smith talked to the friends and associates of Bill they, unsurprisingly, used words such as 'decent', 'honest' and 'trustworthy' to describe him. Essentially similar terms were also used by the criminal associates of Dave who also saw him as 'reliable' and 'trustworthy'. Anderson and Smith conclude that: 'we need to critically examine these relational words . . . Ethics may indicate what is right in any given context but cannot tell us if the context itself is moral' (p. 493). In other words, moral standards or norms may differ between social and economic contexts.

To understand the extent to which the morality of particular activities is socially constructed – i.e. depends on the local institutional context – it is useful to consider rather extreme examples. One notable result of the institutional breakdown in Somalia, for example, which has involved intense violence, ineffectual governance and economic and political instability, has been the emergence of enterprising gangs of Somali pirates (Floyd, 2010). Condemned by international law it is interesting to conjecture to what extent the emergence of the pirates has been a result of the breakdown of institutions and to what extent the result of individual avarice or lack of morality. Certainly, if we are to believe Sugule Ali, a spokesman for the group of Somali pirates who in 2008 raided the cargo ship *Faina*, institutional factors resulting in hunger are major 'push' factors in encouraging people to become pirates. Other evidence from *The New York Times* may also suggest the importance of other factors in reducing other economic options (Box 9.2).

Family background is also a potentially important element of an individual's institutional environment in shaping 'career' choices. It is a well-recognized feature

BOX 9.2   SUGULE ALI – SOMALI PIRATE

On 25 September 2008 the *Faina*, a cargo ship, was raided by a band of around 50 pirates off the Somali coast. The boat was carrying 33 Russian-built battle tanks and crates of grenade launchers, anti-aircraft guns, ammunition and other explosives. After its hijack the ship turned northwards to reach the coastal pirate hideout at Eyl in North-Eastern Somalia. Sugule Ali – a spokesman for the pirates – commented:

'We don't want these weapons to go to anyone in Somalia. Somalia has suffered from many years of destruction because of all these weapons. We don't want that suffering and chaos to continue. We are not going to offload the weapons. We just want the money.'

Asked: 'What will you do with the money?' Sugule Ali responded: 'We will protect ourselves from hunger. We're not afraid of arrest or death or any of these things. For us, hunger is our enemy.'

The New York Times also reported that:

Several fishermen along the Gulf of Aden talked about seeing barrels of toxic waste bobbing in the middle of the ocean. They spoke of clouds of dead fish floating nearby and rogue fishing trawlers sucking up not just fish and lobsters but also the coral and the plants that sustain them. It was abuses like these, several men said, that turned them from fishermen into pirates.

Sources: *The New York Times*, 30 November 2008,
'Somalia's Pirates Flourish in a Lawless Nation'; and
'Q&A with a Pirate: We just want the money'

of the small business literature, for example, that entrepreneurship runs in families – children from families where the parents have run businesses are much more likely to become business owners in their own right (Colombier and Masclet, 2008). The example of Sandra Avila Beltran provides a colourful example of how this can work in the context of antisocial enterprise (Box 9.3).

Research such as that by Anderson and Smith (2007) and the case studies outlined in this section emphasize the strongly contextual nature of much crime and individuals' decisions to become engaged in criminal enterprise. In the next section we focus on how researchers have sought to conceptualize the decision to become a criminal entrepreneur.

BOX 9.3   SANDRA AVILA BELTRAN – 'QUEEN OF THE PACIFIC'

Sandra Avila, aka 'The Queen of the Pacific', was born into the Mexican drugs trade, the niece of two convicted Mexican drug traffickers currently serving time in the US. In what was allegedly a colourful criminal career, Sandra was married to two senior police officers – both of whom were subsequently murdered by gunmen – and had a long-term relationship with Juan Diego Espinosa, a central figure in the Mexican drugs trade. US prosecutors reportedly said: 'Along the way she seduced many drug kingpins and upper echelon police officers becoming a powerful force in the cocaine world through a combination of ruthless business sense, a mobster's wiles and her sex appeal.' Allegedly working with Espinosa, prosecutors say that Sandra Avila played an important role in linking Mexican drug traffickers to Colombian suppliers bringing together the Sinaloa gang and Colombia's Norte del Valle cartel. Sandra Avila managed these relationships and, allegedly, set up related legitimate businesses to launder money. Avila was arrested in September 2007 in Mexico City and charged with drug smuggling with the aim of extradition to the US. She was acquitted in December 2010 by a Mexican judge of the majority of the charges against her but remained in custody in Mexico on more minor charges.

Sources: *The Scotsman*, 14 October 2007, 'Why Mexicans get a kick from the cocaine queen'; *Guardian*: International, 6 October 2007, 'Queen of the Pacific has Mexico Hooked'; *Miami Herald*, 3 December 2010, 'Mexican judge absolves reputed drug cartel "queen"'

9.3 CONCEPTUAL PERSPECTIVES

Becker (1968) adopts an economic – utility-based – perspective on criminal enterprise arguing that a person will commit a criminal offence if the expected utility of this activity is greater than that in other alternatives. In essence the decision rule which Becker is suggesting here is the same as that suggested by Blanchflower and Oswald (1998), for whether or not an individual chooses to become an entrepreneur (see Section 5.3). Becker's 'rational theory' of crime suggests in particular that the probability of offending will increase when either the returns increase or the risks fall. In a recent survey, Baker and Piquero (2010), find significant evidence supporting Becker's contention 'that the perceived benefits of offending are significantly associated with criminal offending' (p. 986).

Becker's theory deals with the choice of the individual in whether or not to engage in criminal activity from an economic perspective. Other writers have adopted a more sociological perspective. Smith (1980), for example, emphasizes the development in theories of organized crime in the USA, reflecting a shift since the 1920s in the increasing importance placed on individual agency and the decreasing importance of structure or institutional context (Anderson and Smith, 2007). In the 1920s, Smith (1980) argues, the gangster was seen very much as 'a product of his surroundings in the same way in which a good citizen is a product of his environment' (Smith, 1980, p. 359). This places the emphasis clearly on the institutional context within which individuals are located (Landesco, 1929). In contrast, by the late 1940s studies of the Mafia and the Cosa Nostra emphasize an 'alien' model in which organized crime groups are seen as separate and distinct from society. In the 1960s, Smith (1980) argues, organized crime began to be considered as 'business enterprises organized for the purpose of economic gain through illegal activities' (Clinard and Quinney, 1967, p. 382). This approach emphasizes individual agency and choice, and Smith (1980, p. 371) argues that there exists a

> spectrum of enterprise [that] enables the analyst to perceive instead that the businessman of impeccable standards, the sharp or questionable operator, and the underworld supplier are all entrepreneurs who must be distinguished on grounds other than a master trait of 'criminal'. The loan shark is a credit establishment; the fence is a retailer.

Where an individual business is situated on the spectrum of enterprise activity from the 'very saintly to the most sinful' will depend, Smith (1980) argues, both on the institutional setting and the agency of individual entrepreneurs and consumers. Institutional factors such as law and regulation, for example, may determine whether an individual business operates legally or illegally, something which may differ between countries. In the Netherlands, for example, some coffee

109

shops also sell small amounts of cannabis for immediate consumption; in the majority of other European countries such activity can only operate 'underground'. Other regulatory factors may also influence whether businesses operate legally or in the informal sector with entrepreneurs' choice reflecting the costs and benefits of legitimacy compared with those of operating informally (Box 3.2). Djankov *et al.* (2002a), however, differentiate between unofficial and subsistence enterprises. Unofficial enterprises are those which result from a desire to avoid the administrative or cost burden of state regulation, while subsistence enterprises are the result of coping strategies adopted by households as a response to unemployment or other economic contingencies.

As in the cases of Bill and Dave discussed by Anderson and Smith (2007), individual agency also plays an important part in where on the spectrum of enterprise activity individuals operate. Individual entrepreneurs may or may not consider illegal activities as part of their personal options (see Boxes 9.2 and 9.3). Customers may also, through choice or necessity, deal with either legal or illegal enterprises. For example, poorer people with few formal banking options may, perforce, use unregulated market services such as moneylenders, or loan sharks. Stenning *et al.* (2010), for example, highlight the growth of unregulated lending in the cities of Krakow, Poland and Bratislava, Slovakia and the high cost of such borrowing. One of their interviewees commented:

> You will have 100,000 crowns and will have to give him 50,000 crowns for arranging the credit, but you will have to pay the whole 150,000 crowns back, plus interest! . . . And each month you have to pay, it depends, 2,000 or 3,000 crowns plus interest.
>
> (Stenning *et al.*, 2010, p. 140)

What then determines the position on the spectrum of enterprise activity which any business adopts? In the context of underground enterprises at least, Albanese (2000) provides a model which can be used to predict the prevalence of a specific criminal activity and potential harm. Based on a series of case studies of organized crime groups Albanese's model reflects the relationship between criminal opportunities, the criminal environment and the skills required to carry out organized crime. The model is not intended to predict the probability that any specific individual will engage in antisocial enterprise but does aim to reflect the impact which institutional factors will have on the probability of organized crime emerging in a particular product or service market (Figure 9.1).

The value of the Albanese model can be usefully illustrated by considering two brief applications. In Willis (2003), for example, we find a description of the emergence of a range of illicit, unregulated alcoholic 'new generation' drinks in Kenya during the 1990s. Sold cheaply in bars as 'traditional', these drinks proved competitive with more traditional beer which was expensive due to high duties.

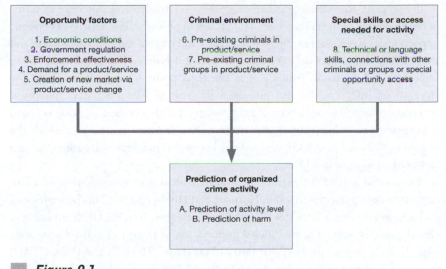

Figure 9.1

Albanese (2000) model for predicting organized crime

Source: Adapted from Albanese (2000), Figure 1.

The origins and safety of many of these new generation drinks were uncertain with concerns about their use of industrial alcohol and some instances of sickness and death after their consumption.

What were the opportunity factors which lay behind the development of these drinks (Albanese, 2000)? First, economic conditions in terms of low average incomes in Kenya and increasing duty on beer created a potential market opportunity and a ready demand. Established bars also provided a ready route to market. Government regulation was also unclear with the local distilling activities of traditional crop-based spirits widely tolerated. As Willis comments: 'The whole story of illicit drinking in Kenya in the 1990s, reveals one of the most striking aspects of crime in modern Africa: that there may be widespread uncertainty as to whether an activity is criminal or not' (Willis, 2003, p. 242). This uncertainty and the toleration of more traditional locally distilled spirits which were sold informally shaped the criminal environment. Key to the development of these new generation drinks, however, were specialist skills and specific opportunities. First, the tradition of distilling in rural areas of Kenya meant there were individuals with skills in making alcoholic drinks. Second, the producers of these drinks were concentrated near Naivasha: 'possibly because it lies on the road along which tankers [travel] carrying industrial alcohol from the sugar refineries of western Kenya to Nairobi' (Willis, 2003, p. 254). The suspicion was that some of the industrial alcohol was being diverted en route to the capital. Innovation was also required, however, as producers tried to find ways to remove markers and poisons from the industrial alcohol they were using.

111

In this case, the Albanese model suggests a relatively clear outcome in terms of the likelihood of the emergence of significant organized crime activity. Economic opportunities were evident; there was a ready and established route to market and those living along the road between Naivasha and Nairobi had good access to an important raw material. Ambiguity in the legal position, and doubts about the strength of enforcement, also increased the risk of illegal activity. Individual enterprise was still necessary to take advantage of these conditions, however, and it is clear from Willis (2003) that many of the criminal enterprises which did engage in this market quickly adopted market norms in terms of labelling, pricing and marketing their products.

The central role of the entrepreneurial individual is more evident in a case of cigarette bootlegging described in Hornsby and Hobbs (2007). This paper focuses on Jason and his firm's activities in cigarette bootlegging into the UK from Europe. (Bootlegging is defined as the 'illegal importation of cigarettes and tobacco after legal duties have been paid in the country of purchase' (Hornsby and Hobbs, 2007, p. 551)). In terms of the Albanese (2000) model, the economic opportunity for cigarette bootlegging to the UK was created by particularly high UK tax rates on cigarettes and ambiguous customs regulations which allowed tax free importation of cigarettes for personal use. Jason and his firm responded by providing UK pensioners with free trips to Europe with all passengers bringing back their maximum free tobacco allowance for Jason. Eventually, encouraged by ineffective enforcement, Jason and his firm moved on to establish a new operation in France, to wholesale cigarettes originally purchased in Luxembourg to other people bootlegging cigarettes into the UK. In this way Jason was able to sell cigarettes at above the Luxembourg price and below the French price, giving him a margin and increasing the profit margins of the bootleggers. This operation – seen as relatively low-risk by the firm – depended on there being other criminal 'customers' for the service, or what Albanese (2000) called the criminal environment. In setting up this operation, Jason showed considerable organizational and entrepreneurial skills. Hornsby and Hobbs comment: We can 'regard these actors as entrepreneurs working on a constantly shifting terrain of profit-rich consumer markets, the barriers between legal and illegal entrepreneurship become permanently blurred' (Hornsby and Hobbs, 2007, p. 559). Here again, we see evidence of each element of the Albanese framework, a combination of economic opportunity, a criminal environment and Jason's entrepreneurial skills and criminal networks.

9.4 SUMMARY AND KEY POINTS

Antisocial enterprise can vary from the purely informal to the plain evil. In each case, however, the motivations and the activities involved are likely to reflect relatively closely those in more mainstream entrepreneurship. Opportunity recognition, resource gathering and coordination and risk-taking are common to both suggesting that they can be represented on a spectrum of enterprise activity (Smith, 1980). Others would argue that antisocial entrepreneurship may be functionally similar to mainstream enterprise but is morally different. Or, at least as Anderson and Smith (2007) suggest, that notions of entrepreneurship are socially constructed and that these social constructions often have a moral element endowing 'entrepreneurship' with positive social or economic properties.

Neo-institutional perspectives recognize the importance of agency and the capacity of the individual entrepreneur for 'institutional work', i.e. the capacity to change institutions either for good or ill. Models such as that developed by Albanese (2000) emphasize institutions, and their effect on the likelihood that organized crime will develop in a particular economic and social context. However, without an understanding of how such institutions influence agency, and outcomes in turn influence institutions, such models remain rather incomplete compared to more fully developed models of conventional entrepreneurship (Lu and Tao, 2010).

9.5 DISCUSSION QUESTIONS AND FURTHER READING

The moral status of entrepreneurship is explored thoroughly in Anderson and Smith (2007) which is a dense but excellent read. Albanese (2000) provides an insightful view of the causes of crime while Djankov *et al.* (2002a) deal with the issue of informal enterprise. Papers by Hornsby and Hobbs (2007) and Pearson and Hobbs (2003) in the criminology literature emphasize the socially embedded nature of antisocial or criminal enterprise.

This chapter suggests the following discussion questions:

1 Can drug-dealing be entrepreneurial? Or, does entrepreneurship have to be more socially 'positive'?
2 Is criminal enterprise driven by necessity or opportunity?
3 What else would you want to add to the Albanese model for predicting organized crime (Figure 9.1)? Are there other important factors?

Chapter 10

Enterprise policy

10.1 INTRODUCTION

Almost every country in the world has a set of policy measures directed at small business or entrepreneurship. Why is this? What is this policy intervention trying to achieve? In this chapter we focus on the rationale and justification for government intervention to support entrepreneurship and small firms, outline the alternative policy options which governments have adopted and report some indicators of success. Underpinning the discussion is the economic notion of 'market failure' and its implication that without government intervention levels of welfare – reflected perhaps in national GDP – will be lower than with intervention. This leads to a consideration of the wide range of policy options which governments have to consider when supporting small firms. For example, is it sufficient for government to shape the framework conditions within which entrepreneurs operate or are there groups of firms – or potential entrepreneurs – which require more targeted support?

For most countries, policy intervention in entrepreneurship and SMEs is a permanent element of the policy environment. It can also be expensive. This creates the potential (and the need) for learning about which measures work and which do not, emphasizing the value of policy evaluation. But, how do we assess whether a policy initiative has been a success? Is it enough to consider the immediate impacts of the intervention? Or, do we also have to consider the longer-term social and economic consequences? For example, in many countries entrepreneurship policy has focused on new business formation. Fritsch and Mueller (2004), for example, consider the impact of new business formation on economic growth in German regions and highlight the complexity and time-lags involved in turning new business formation into overall employment gains. This analysis, which considers the impact of new business formation on regional employment growth, suggests three impact phases (Figure 10.1). Over the first couple of years, after new businesses are set up, they do create some new jobs.

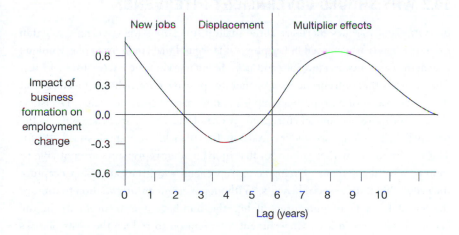

New jobs | Displacement | Multiplier effects

Impact of business formation on employment change

Lag (years)

Figure 10.1
Firm formation and regional employment change

Source: Derived from Fritsch and Muller (2004), Figure 2.

As these businesses grow, however, in years three to five, they out-compete other local firms causing job losses in other firms in the region – so-called 'displacement'. Then, as the new firms then carry on growing they have a positive jobs effect in years six onwards both through the jobs they create directly and also through potential 'multiplier' effects. The results of Fritsch and Mueller (2004) suggest some of the difficulty of policy evaluation; the need to take into account both direct effects and the displacement of existing economic activity as well as multiplier effects; and that the timing of any assessment of policy effects is crucial. In later sections of the chapter we consider the range of approaches which have been adopted to evaluate entrepreneurship policy from simple opinion-based measures, through econometric approaches to more experimental approaches.

The key learning objectives of this chapter are as follows:

- To introduce students to the rationale for government intervention, focusing on notions of market failure and systemic failure.
- To introduce different types of policy intervention to support entre-preneurship and small business and some evidence relating to national priorities.
- To provide students with an understanding of issues and methodologies relating to policy evaluation.

Further reading and discussion questions are included in Section 10.7.

115

10.2 WHY SHOULD GOVERNMENT INTERVENE?

Bennett (2008) argues there are three main justifications for government action for SMEs. First, as we noted in Chapter 3 it is argued that small firms play a unique role in the economy creating jobs and stimulating market renewal (Robson, 1996). This suggests that entrepreneurship generates positive externalities, meaning that the 'social' value of entrepreneurship is greater than its 'private' value. Decisions about whether to become an entrepreneur or not, however, are based only on the private benefits and ignore wider social benefits (Blanchflower and Oswald, 1998). This represents a 'market failure' in that individual entrepreneurs are not able to capture all of the benefits of being an entrepreneur – i.e. they are able to capture the private but not the social benefits. Without government intervention to capture the social benefits of entrepreneurship the number of entrepreneurs in the economy will remain low. Government intervention to reduce the costs or risks of entrepreneurship is, therefore, justified to raise the level of entrepreneurial activity to that closer to the social optimum.

Similar types of market failures also exist which have been suggested as a justification for government intervention to support SME development. For example, SMEs may find it more difficult to obtain finance than larger firms due to a lack of collateral, their unproven track record and the proportionally greater cost of small transactions (see Chapter 7). SMEs may also find it more difficult to adopt new technologies than larger firms due to their greater need to use external technologies but their weaker internal technical resources (see Chapter 8). In each case, the 'market failure' might justify government intervention to support SME lending, to help small firms adopt new technologies or perhaps provide SMEs with marketing or export information.

These arguments about market failure stem largely from neoclassical economics, which some have argued provides only a weak basis for real world policy making (Metcalfe, 1997). Other perspectives, based on evolutionary economics, provide a different type of justification for policy intervention, arguing that government can develop a strategic vision for the economy or a particular sector which individual SMEs cannot (Bennett, 2008). In the early development of renewable energy markets, for example, government intervention has repeatedly been shown to be important in stimulating demand and promoting sectoral development. In the case of wind energy, in particular, government intervention has often been important both to stimulate demand and entrepreneurial engagement with the emerging sector (Buen, 2006, Perez and Ramos-Real, 2009). Government may also see other types of strategic priorities such as supporting high-tech firms (Avnimelech *et al.*, 2007), women's entrepreneurship (Meurs *et al.*, 2008) or entrepreneurship among disadvantaged or ethnic minority groups (Scott and Irwin, 2009). In each case, the policy justification is likely to be strategic – or social – rather than depending on some narrowly defined 'market failure'.

10.3 WHAT TYPE OF POLICY INTERVENTION?

Once a decision has been made that a government should intervene to support entrepreneurship or small business development the next question is what type of intervention is appropriate? The first decision to be made is at what 'level' intervention should take place. Autio *et al.* (2007) make a useful distinction between four 'levels' of policy intervention: (1) macro-economic conditions; (2) framework conditions; (3) mainstream SME support measures; and (4) targeted support measures:

- Macro-economic conditions – these set the national context for business development and include issues related to economic stability and growth, national legislative frameworks, and social and political stability. Uncertainty about either future growth or policy continuity, for example, may undermine individuals' willingness to invest (Bhattacharjee *et al.*, 2009, Norberg-Bohm, 2000).

- Framework conditions – these provide the more specific context for entrepreneurship and small business and relate, for example, to resource and factor availability, regulation, legislation and property rights as well as transport, environmental and legislatory systems. It is at this level that framework conditions in developing (Bruton *et al.*, 2009) and transition economies (Groh and von Liechtenstein, 2009) may often discourage investment and/or risk-taking.

- Mainstream SME support – this relates to broadly based policy initiatives targeted to support entrepreneurship and small business. This would include measures to support enterprise culture and enterprise education (Box 10.1) as well as business and advice centres, and grants, loans or guarantees aimed specifically at SMEs (Boxes 7.2 and 7.3).

- Targeted SME measures – these relate to narrowly focused initiatives intended to support the development of a particular group of entrepreneurs or small firms. Examples would be support offered to women's enterprise through specialist advice services and business centres (Box 10.2) and to high-tech firms through science parks, business incubators and accelerators (Boxes 6.4 and 6.5).

Even this is not the end of the story, however, as governments also have to decide at which point in the life-cycle of the business to intervene, or at least how to divide their resources between supporting start-ups or supporting growing businesses. Promoting start-up is popular with local development agencies (Johnson, 2005) but may be wasteful if start-ups are of poor quality (Storey and Johnson, 1986) and it simply promotes wasteful churn.

BOX 10.1 SUPPORTING THE MAINSTREAM – ENTREPRENEURSHIP EDUCATION

The EU Oslo Agenda (2006) for Entrepreneurship Education aims to integrate entrepreneurship education into each stage of the educational process. This type of initiative is generally supported by well-established and documented examples of experience and good practice at both schools and universities. Two examples of best practice illustrate this point. First, a framework established by the Norwegian government provides a national policy agenda which sets out clear objectives and progression in enterprise education across all stages of students' education. Second, the University of Waterloo situated at the heart of Canada's Technology Triangle provides an outstanding example of an entrepreneurial university. Strongly embedded within the regional community, dense cooperative networks on technology and enterprise between the university and the local community are complemented by the university's cooperative education programme. 'The rotation of students to industry and back to the classroom solidified already tight relations with local industry. The reflexive relationship has allowed the curriculum to keep up with the ever changing technological frontiers of industry' (Bramwell and Wolfe, 2008, p. 1181). Over 250 spin-outs from the university have resulted in part from the university policy of allowing ownership of intellectual property to rest with its creator (faculty or student), encouraging both creativity and enterprise.

Sources: Norwegian directorate for education and training (2006).
'Norwegian Strategy Plan for Entrepreneurship in Education',
Oslo, Norwegian directorate for education and training;
and Bramwell and Wolfe (2008)

BOX 10.2 PROMOTING WOMEN'S ENTERPRISE

Academic opinions differ about whether or not women entrepreneurs have specific development needs. Recent evidence suggests, however, that in the UK at least women do face specific barriers in terms of starting a business (Roper and Scott, 2009). Other evidence suggests that when women do start businesses their companies are more often under-capitalized than those of male entrepreneurs (Coleman, 2007). In many countries this has led to the development of organizations which aim to promote female enterprise by promoting examples of successful women entrepreneurs;

'enabling' women business owners through training; establishing women's business networks; and supporting equality charter schemes. National organizations like Catalyst in the USA, and the Centre of Arab Women for Training and Research in Tunisia are complemented by international organizations such as Womenable.

One key activity undertaken by these national organizations has been the promotion and quality assurance of specialist advice services for women's enterprise. The Prowess Flagship Award in the United Kingdom, for example, was a 'best practice' quality standard for excellence in women's enterprise development. This nationally and internationally recognized quality mark was achieved by organizations all over the UK. Supported by UK government departments and regional agencies, the Flagship Award incorporated three quality mark standards for start-up support, support for established businesses and support for women's business networks. Local organizations working towards the Flagship Award were able to access national expertise to help develop their business support and advice services. This led to completion of a self-assessment document and assessment visit before Flagship status was awarded. Periodic reviews of support procedures and personnel were then required for renewal of the award.

The research evidence also suggests that for women entrepreneurs women-only networks can be very important during the establishment phase with online networks playing an increasingly important role (e.g. http://www. giantpotential.com). Broader networks are needed for growth, however. The Center for Women & Enterprise (CWE), Massachusetts, USA, for example, runs a broad range of networking events organized along cultural and aspirational lines and intended to provide a menu of options from which women entrepreneurs can select depending on the stage of development of their business and their aspiration. These include: monthly women's networking events; 'Coffee and Capital' equity breakfasts for women and local financiers; 'Destination Success' – an annual network event bringing together new and successful women entrepreneurs; and Latina entre-preneurs' networking events. CWE also offer other services intended to help female entrepreneurs to grow their businesses. These include an online business directory to assist with marketing and a comprehensive series of training courses for women 'envisioning' and 'growing' their businesses.

Sources: Catalyst, http://www.catalyst.org;
Centre of Arab Women for Training and Research,
http://www.cawtar.org;
Womenable, http://www.womenable.com;
CWE, http://cweonline.org

10.4 FRAMEWORK CONDITIONS

As we have already noted, neo-institutional perspectives suggest the importance of the economic, legal and regulatory frameworks within which start-up and growth take place. Reflecting this, international benchmarks have been developed which reflect the framework conditions for business in different countries. Perhaps the most interesting of these is the *Doing Business* report published annually by the World Bank and the International Finance Corporation. Based on regulatory information for different countries and an assessment of the time and cost required to complete certain business activities this currently provides information on framework conditions in 183 countries. Nine areas of the environment for business are covered by the index, focusing on the costs of starting and closing a business and including other issues such as credit availability and the costs of exporting and importing. Aspects of the legislative framework are also covered such as the ease or difficulty of paying taxes, enforcing contracts and property rights (Table 10.1).

The *Doing Business* report is based on a programme of research on the business environment in different countries conducted by the staff at the World Bank. One of the most influential studies was that undertaken by Djankov *et al.* (2002b) who explored the time and costs involved in starting a business in 85 countries. This was seen as important as this regulation can create a barrier to start-up and, in developing economies at least, a potential barrier to formal (rather than informal) business start-up. Djankov and his co-authors use data from a company survey and other official sources to profile the business start-up process in each country. One of their key conclusions was the diversity of the number of regulatory steps needed to start a company: 'The number of procedures required to start up a firm varies from the low of two in Canada to the high of 21 in the Dominican Republic, with the world average of around 10' (Djankov *et al.*, 2002b, p. 4). These differences in the start-up process also lead to a significant difference in the time taken to start a company:

> The minimum official time for such a start-up varies from the low of 2 business days in Australia and Canada to the high of 152 in Madagascar, assuming that there are no delays by either the applicant or the regulators, with the world average of 47 business days.
>
> (Djankov *et al.*, 2002b, p. 4)

In terms of start-up, one of the key findings from the Djankov *et al.*, (2002b) study is that regulation can be very expensive for entrepreneurs: 'For an entrepreneur, legal entry is extremely cumbersome, time-consuming, and expensive in most countries in the world' (Djankov *et al.*, 2002b, p. 4). This regulation may, of course, be rational if in countries where start-up is more difficult churn is lower or the quality of the products and services provided by new firms is higher.

Table 10.1 Elements of the Doing Business index, 2011

Starting a business	Getting credit	Trading across borders
Procedures (number)	Strength of legal rights index (0–10)	Documents to export (number)
Time (days)	Depth of credit information index (0–6)	Time to export (days)
Cost (% of income per capita)	Public registry coverage (% of adults)	Cost to export (US$ per container)
Minimum capital (% of income per capita)	Private bureau coverage (% of adults)	Documents to import (number)
		Time to import (days)
		Cost to import (US$ per container)
Dealing with construction permits	**Protecting investors**	**Enforcing contracts**
Procedures (number)	Extent of disclosure index (0–10)	Procedures (number)
Time (days)	Extent of director liability index (0–10)	Time (days)
Cost (% of income per capita)	Ease of shareholder suits index (0–10)	Cost (% of claim)
	Strength of investor protection index (0–10)	
Registering property	Paying taxes	Closing a business
Procedures (number)	Payments (number per year)	Time (years)
Time (days)	Time (hours per year)	Cost (% of estate)
Cost (% of property value)	Total tax rate (% of profit)	Recovery rate (cents on the dollar)

Source: Doing Business 2011, see: http://www.doingbusiness.org.

Djankov *et al.* (2002b) argue that this is not the case, however, with little evidence that greater regulation is linked to better service or product quality but considerable evidence that greater regulation is linked to higher levels of corruption and a larger informal or unofficial sector. As Djankov *et al.* comment: 'the principal beneficiaries [of higher levels of regulation] seem to be the politicians and bureaucrats themselves' (Djankov *et al.*, 2002b, p. 35).

In the 2011 *Doing Business* report, Singapore comes top of the league table as the easiest place to do business, a position it also held in 2010 (Table 10.2). Other countries in the top ten also tend to be high-income economies with well-developed legal, regulatory and banking systems and also tend to have been in the top ten in the previous year. More generally, OECD high-income countries tend to come closest to the top of the rankings with an average position of 30 (out of

121

Table 10.2 *Ease of doing business – top 10 countries*

Ranking in 2011	Country	Ranking in 2010
1	Singapore	1
2	Hong Kong	2
3	New Zealand	3
4	UK	4
5	US	5
6	Denmark	6
7	Canada	9
8	Norway	7
9	Ireland	8
10	Australia	10

Source: Doing Business 2011, Table 12. See: http://www.doingbusiness.org.

183). Eastern European and Central Asian economies are clustered below the OECD economies with an average position of 72. Just below this group are the East Asia and Pacific economies and a group of countries in Latin America, the Caribbean and the Middle East (average position 96), and below these are some of the South Asian economies (average position 117). Towards the bottom of the table are the countries of sub-Saharan Africa (average position 137), emphasizing the difficulty of the business environment in some of these countries.

Institutional effects on start-up are clearly well documented and this is reflected in the *Doing Business* reports. But how does regulation influence business growth? Capelleras *et al.* (2008) consider this question, comparing firm growth in a highly regulated country – Spain which is 48th in the 2011 *Doing Business* table – and a 'low' regulated economy – the UK – which is 4th. What makes this study particularly interesting is that it is based on survey data from firms in both the formal and the informal economies and reflects both the choice between setting up a business in the formal or the informal sectors and the contrasting growth of each group of firms (Box 3.2). The study suggests two key results. First, Capelleras *et al.* (2008) find support for the point made by Djankov *et al.* (2002b) that higher levels of regulation may restrict formally constituted enterprises – these firms are fewer and grow more slowly in Spain. Overall, however, Capelleras *et al.* (2008) find that regulatory differences make little difference to the overall growth achieved by the formal and informal sectors taken together. The implication is that regulation has little detrimental growth effect on the economy as a whole but will influence the division of economic activity between the formal and the informal sectors. This has important implications of course for tax revenues, employee rights and, potentially, issues such as health and safety.

Doing Business provides an influential and persuasive set of international benchmarks for framework conditions. Indeed, some countries have used their position in the *Doing Business* league tables as an indication of the quality of their business environment, as part of attempts to attract inward investment. In *Investing in Montenegro 2010*, for example, Montenegro highlights both its progress in reforming the business environment and its improving position in the *Doing Business* league tables (http://www.developingmarkets.com). For other countries, such as the transition economies of Eastern and Central Europe, the *Doing Business* report provides an influential driver for organizational and regulatory reform.

10.5 EVALUATING ENTREPRENEURSHIP POLICY

Whatever form of entrepreneurship policy is adopted in a particular country a key question is whether the policy has 'worked', or more precisely whether it has achieved its aims and objectives. For example, has the intervention helped the type of firms it was intended to help? Or, has it been monopolized by other types of firms? Has the management of the initiative been adequate and cost-effective in supporting the intervention? Scheme evaluations attempt to answer this type of question, provide an assessment of the effectiveness of an intervention and, in most cases, some recommendations for how an initiative might be improved. A number of concepts are central to any evaluation project:

- The 'counterfactual' – this is essentially what would have happened without the intervention. So, the difference between the counterfactual and what actually happened is the impact of the intervention. Counterfactuals are often difficult to identify, with much effort afforded to different analytical approaches to identify them.
- The term 'additionality' is used to reflect the extent to which a targeted policy initiative has a measurable effect on the target companies. Full additionality is said to occur where the policy initiative causes the firm to do something which it would not have done in the absence of the support. Zero additionality occurs where the policy initiative has no effect on the activities of the firm. This is also sometimes called 'deadweight'. The intermediate case – partial additionality – occurs where an initiative has some more marginal impact on a firm's activities, perhaps encouraging it to undertake an activity more quickly or at a larger scale than it would have done in the absence of the policy measure.
- Displacement and multiplier effects may also be important in assessing the impact of some policy initiatives as the study by Fritsch and Mueller (2004) suggests.

Entrepreneurship policy evaluations take a number of forms, and Potter and Storey (2007) provide a very useful review of evaluation best practice across the OECD.

123

At the centre of their approach is what they call the 'six steps' of evaluation, with each step representing an increase in the sophistication of the evaluation method. The key idea is that at each 'step' the counterfactual is better defined and so the impact or additionality of the policy initiative can be more accurately measured. Steps 1 to 3 in the Potter and Storey (2007) evaluation schema are sometimes called 'monitoring measures':

- Step 1 involves measuring the take-up of any scheme by potential users. This provides some information on the popularity of the measure and at least an indication of the scheme's potential impact. Where take-up is low, impacts are also likely to be low. This type of monitoring can usually be conducted using scheme management data and typically requires no new data collection.
- Step 2 involves measuring recipient opinion of the scheme. This again provides information on the popularity of the measure and some indication of whether it was found valuable. Gathering this type of information may require new data collection from scheme recipients. Potter and Storey (2007, Table 2.10) cite the example of Investment Readiness support measures in New Zealand as an example of Step 2 evaluation.
- Step 3 involves measuring views of the difference made by the scheme. As it is often cost-effective, this is a very popular form of evaluation, but clearly relies on the subjective assessments of scheme recipients. These assessments may be positively biased either because recipients have benefited from the scheme in the past or because they hope to benefit again from it in the future (Fraser *et al.*, 2007). Again this type of evaluation often requires gathering new data from scheme recipients.
- The Step 4 to Step 6 evaluation approaches outlined by Potter and Storey (2007) each require more extensive new data collection than the Step 1 to Step 3 approaches and are more expensive and time-consuming to implement. Thus, there is a trade-off between the extra information they provide and the costs/time involved.
- Step 4 evaluations compare the performance of firms 'assisted' by a scheme and the performance of 'typical' firms. Here the performance of the 'typical' firms is taken as the counterfactual, and the difference between the performance of the assisted and typical groups is said to be the effect of the scheme. The key advantage over a Step 3 evaluation is that scheme effects are measured differences rather than subjective assessments; the downside is that this type of approach does not control for differences in the characteristics of assisted and typical firms. This is important because these characteristics – including perhaps the ambition of the entrepreneur or owner-manager – may themselves be a cause of differences in performance, causing performance differences between the assisted and typical group to be wrongly attributed to the impact of the scheme.

- Step 5 evaluations are intended to overcome this attribution problem by comparing the performance of the 'assisted' group with the performance of a control group of similar matched firms. Typically, however, such matches take into account the size, sector, and perhaps location of the assisted and control groups but still cannot take into account other, less readily observable, differences between the characteristics of the assisted and control groups of firms. Again the potential exists for performance differences between the assisted and the control group to be misattributed to the intervention.

- Step 6 evaluations – which Potter and Storey (2007) regard as 'best practice', go further and attempt to take account of what is generally called selection bias. For example, selection bias can arise because 'better' or 'more ambitious' firms might seek support and hence bias upwards the results of any Step 5 type scheme evaluation. Alternatively, a policy measure might be targeted at under-performing firms, again biasing any control group type assessment of scheme impacts. Correcting for this type of selection bias typically involves collecting detailed survey data from both an assisted and a control group of firms, and then a rather complex two-part econometric approach: the first part models the impact of the characteristics of firms on the probability that they received support from the scheme; the second then models the actual impact of the support, controlling for the impact of characteristics differences. For an early example of this type of evaluation see Roper and Hewitt-Dundas (2001).

Econometric approaches to evaluation such as the Step 6 approaches advocated by Potter and Storey (2007) have a number of advantages: they offer a formal and transparent way of controlling for selection bias; they allow other performance drivers to be taken into account; and they provide a quantifiable estimate of policy impacts. The disadvantages of this type of econometric *ex post* evaluation are also significant, however:

- They are very data intensive requiring detailed survey data on a large group of assisted and non-assisted firms. Relatively large samples are needed to allow the quite complex econometric models to be appropriately estimated.
- There is a need to allow for an 'impact period' over which the effects of the policy can be observed and measured. This means that the results of this type of evaluation are not available till some time (perhaps two to three years) after the intervention.

So is there a different approach? Well arguably there is, although it suggests a rather different policy-making approach to that traditionally adopted. The policy evaluation approaches outlined in Potter and Storey (2007) are all '*ex post*' techniques. In other words, the evaluation occurs after the implementation of the

125

BOX 10.3 EVALUATING CREATIVE CREDITS

Creative Credits are business-to-business innovation vouchers being piloted in the North West of England around Manchester. The scheme enables SMEs to buy around £5,000 ($7,900) of input from a creative services or design business to help develop their innovation activity. This policy experiment involves a randomized controlled trial (RCT) with vouchers being randomly allocated between applicant SMEs rather than being allocated on the basis of, say, the quality of the submitted projects. Adopting this random allocation approach avoids potential selection bias in assessing the impacts of the scheme rather than having to 'correct' for potential selection bias. The adoption of an RCT approach does have potential welfare implications, however. In the short term, the trade-off is between the potential welfare gains from a targeted provision of support and that which would arise from a random lottery-based allocation. In the longer term this short-term cost should be offset by the gains from the more effective evaluation.

Initial results from the evaluation of the Creative Credits scheme suggest no systemic differences in the characteristics of the recipient and non-recipient groups. This suggests the validity of the RCT approach. Early evaluation results are also positive, suggesting significant short-term additionality.

Source: Bakhshi *et al.* (2011)

policy. The risk is that the policy is ineffective, potentially wasting significant amounts of public money before it is evaluated. An alternative approach is some form of *ex ante* or experimental evaluation in which the effect of the policy is 'tested' in a controlled setting. Box 10.3 describes one such experiment relating to the UK evaluation of Creative Credits.

10.6 SUMMARY AND KEY POINTS

As the material in this chapter has suggested debates about the role and value of specific entrepreneurship and small business policies continue. What is the best focus of policy – start-ups or growing firms? Should policy be regional or national? Should it be targeted at industries or specific groups of entrepreneurs or firms? How should we decide between these alternatives? What is generally agreed, however, is that compared to larger firms, small firms and entrepreneurs do face particular problems and that this justifies some targeted policy intervention. At its most limited this may simply be simpler or less demanding regulation for small companies; in other countries more active interventions can be found with support targeted, for example, at high-growth firms. There is also general agreement that if we are going to have a small business policy then understanding and evaluating its effects is important. How this evaluation should be done, however, remains a contentious issue (Tsai and Kuo, 2011).

10.7 DISCUSSION QUESTIONS AND FURTHER READING

On the alternative types of policy intervention to support entrepreneurship and high-tech growth see Autio *et al.* (2007). Evaluation of small business policy is considered in detail in Potter and Storey (2007).

This chapter suggests the following discussion questions:

1   What is the most important type of market failure for small firms which might justify government intervention to support entrepreneurs?
2   How should the government intervene? At what level?
3   Should the govenment focus support on encouraging start-up or supporting growth? How would you decide which was most effective?

Chapter 11

Looking forwards

Research on entrepreneurship around the globe has developed rapidly in recent years supported by projects such as the GEM initiative and rapid growth in other national and international data sources. One of the key insights from these projects has been the extent to which entrepreneurship activity varies, with levels generally higher in developing and transition economies. It is also suggested by evidence from the GEM project, however, that in some richer countries (US, Hong Kong, Iceland) higher levels of entrepreneurial activity are, at least, associated with higher levels of income. A key question for the future therefore is whether rapidly developing countries can continue their economic development and maintain high levels of entrepreneurial activity as a stimulus to further growth. The alternative, that levels of entrepreneurial activity decline as development continues, is perhaps more likely. For these countries, therefore, shaping the institutional and policy environment to sustain high levels of entrepreneurial activity will be important. Key elements of this are likely to be the legal restrictions around firm ownership (Djankov *et al.*, 2002a), the financial system (Beck *et al.*, 2008a), and the framework conditions for business growth (Autio *et al.*, 2007). More direct policy intervention may also be important both to maximize the potential synergies between different enablers of entrepreneurial activity (Avnimelech *et al.*, 2007) and to 'create advantage' through developments in the innovation system (Cooke and Leydesdorff, 2006).

Equally important as the need to maintain levels of entrepreneurial or start-up activity, however, may be the need to support the 'right' types of entrepreneurial activity. As the evidence in Chapter 3 suggests, national growth depends on job creation in smaller firms (Ayyagari *et al.*, 2011) while job creation in smaller firms depends crucially on the gazelles (Henrekson and Johansson, 2010). Supporting such firms, or at least providing an environment within which gazelles can flourish, is a central policy challenge. To date, perhaps due to data constraints, there has been relatively little research on the nature of fast growing companies in developing and transition economies – a key research topic for the future.

One of the other key themes suggested by the research reviewed in earlier chapters is the strongly contextual nature of entrepreneurial activity. From a research standpoint this requires the development of more multi-level analyses of entrepreneurial behaviour reflecting individual (agentic) influences but also the effects of the institutional context (structure). An interesting issue, for example, is the relative importance of structural and agentic influences on entrepreneurship in different international contexts. Similarly, how important are these influences for different types of entrepreneurial actors, e.g. women, young people, immigrant groups? Two other related issues are important. First, how do different elements of the institutional structure of an economy come together or interact to influence entrepreneurial activity? Avnimelech *et al.* (2007), for example, emphasize the synergy between business incubation and the availability of business finance while Buys and Mbewana (2007) emphasize the relationship between business incubation success and access to the science base. These institutional complementarities provide an interesting focus for future research, potentially reflecting the value of a systemic approach to any consideration of institutional effects on entrepreneurship.

A second issue suggested by a multi-level approach to understanding entrepreneurship is the interaction between individuals' entrepreneurial behaviour and institutional structure. Individuals' decisions about business start-up, for example, might create a demonstration effect for other potential entrepreneurs. Or new start-ups might change the availability of specialist services in a particular locality which may itself stimulate new start-up activity. Researching either of these issues or similar dynamic processes is likely to require a longitudinal approach. Essentially similar considerations might apply to further research which tries to explore the consequences of entrepreneurial activity for job creation, innovation or cohesion. Here both longitudinal and comparative perspectives would be valuable, focusing on the temporal and the situational factors which shape the results of entrepreneurship outcomes. How, for example, are the growth implications of entrepreneurship moderated by the availability of bank finance, criminality, etc.?

Finally, it is worth noting that the limitations of current research on entrepreneurship are not only empirical. Received conceptual perspectives on entrepreneurship continue to be dominated by the North Atlantic experience and shaped by the cultural and institutional context of Europe and North America. Huge scope exists for conceptual development to aid our understanding of entrepreneurial behaviour in different national and cultural contexts. Hopefully the material in this book may stimulate some new thinking in this area.

References

Abou-Gabal, N., Khwaja, A. I. and Klinger, B. 2011. *Islamic Finance and Entrepreneurship: Challenges and opportunities ahead.* Harvard University, Entrepreneurial Finance Lab Research Initiative, Centre for International Development, Islamic Finance Whitepaper.

Acs, Z. and Mueller, P. 2008. Employment effects of business dynamics: Mice, gazelles and elephants. *Small Business Economics,* 30, 85–100.

Advisory Committee on Measuring Innovation in the 21st Century Economy 2008. Innovation measurement – Tracking the state of innovation in the US economy. *A report to the Secretary of Commerce.* Available at http://www.esa.doc.gov/sites/default/files/reports/documents/innovation_measurement_01-08.pdf

Aernoudt, R., San Josæ, A. and Roure, J. 2007. Public support for the business angel market in Europe – A critical review. *Venture Capital,* 9, 71–84.

Aggarwal, R. K. and Yousef, T. 2000. Islamic banks and investment financing. *Journal of Money Credit and Banking,* 32, 93–120.

Aidis, R., Welter, F., Smallbone, D. and Isakova, N. 2007. Female entrepreneurship in transition economies: The case of Lithuania and Ukraine. *Feminist Economics,* 13, 157–83.

Albanese, J. S. 2000. The causes of organized crime: Do criminals organize around opportunities for crime or do criminal opportunities create new offenders? *Journal of Contemporary Criminal Justice,* 16, 409–23.

Aldrich, H. E. 1999. *Organizations Evolving.* London, Sage.

Allen, B. and Udell, G. 2006. A more complete conceptual framework for SME financing. *Journal of Banking and Finance,* 30, 11, 2945–66.

Anderson, A. R. and Smith, R. 2007. The moral space in entrepreneurship: An exploration of ethical imperatives and the moral legitimacy of being enterprising. *Entrepreneurship and Regional Development,* 19, 479–97.

Anyadike-Danes, M., Bonner, K., Hart, M. and Mason, C. 2009. *Measuring Business Growth: High growth firms and their contribution to employment in the UK.* London, NESTA.

Audretsch, D. B. 1998. Agglomeration and the location of innovative activity. *Oxford Review of Economic Policy,* 14, 18–29.

—— 2002. The dynamic role of small firms: Evidence from the U.S. *Small Business Economics,* 18, 13–40.

—— 2005. The knowledge spillover theory of entrepreneurship and economic growth in Vinig, G. T. and Van Der Voort, R. C. (eds) *The Emergence of Entrepreneurial Economics*. Oxford, Elsevier.

—— 2007. *Entrepreneurship, Innovation and Economic Growth*. Cheltenham, Edward Elgar.

Autio, E., Kronlund, M. and Kovalainen, A. 2007. *High-Growth SME Support Initiatives in Nine Countries: Analysis, categorization, and recommendations*. Helsinki, Report for the Ministry of Trade and Industry.

Avnimelech, G., Schwartz, D. and Bar-El, R. 2007. Entrepreneurial high-tech cluster development: Israel's experience with venture capital and technological incubators. *European Planning Studies,* 15, 1181–98.

Ayyagari, M., Demirguc-Kunt, A. and Maksimovi, V. 2011. Small vs young firms across the world: Contribution to employment, job creation and growth. Washington DC, *World Bank Working Paper*.

Baker, T. and Piquero, A. R. 2010. Assessing the perceived benefits–criminal offending relationship. *Journal of Criminal Justice,* 38, 981–7.

Bakhshi, H., Edwards, J., Roper, S., Scully, J. and Shaw, D. 2011. Bridging the divide: Using innovation vouchers to link SMEs and creative service providers – first results from a UK mixed-methods evaluation. *Evaluating Innovation Policy, Methods and Applications*, Florence, EUNIP Workshop.

Barkham, R., Gudgin, G., Hart, M. and Hanvey, E. 1996. *The Determinants of Small Firm Growth: An inter-regional study in the UK 1986–90*. London, Jessica Kingsley.

Barney, J. B. 1986. Strategic factor markets – Expectations, luck, and business strategy. *Management Science,* 32, 1230–41.

Baumol, W. J. 2002. *The Free Market Innovation Machine*. Princeton, Princeton University Press.

Beck, T., Demirguc-Kunt, A. and Maksimovic, V. 2008a. Financing patterns around the world: Are small firms different? *Journal of Financial Economics,* 89, 467–87.

Beck, T., Klapper, L. F. and Mendoza, J. C. 2008b. The typology of partial credit guarantee funds around the world. Washington DC, World Bank.

Becker, G. S. 1968. Crime and punishment: An economic approach. *Journal of Political Economy,* 76, 169–217.

Bennett, R. 2008. SME policy support in Britain since the 1990s: What have we learnt? *Environment and Planning C: Government and Policy,* 26, 375–97.

Bhattacharjee, A., Higson, C., Holly, S. and Kattumanw, P. 2009. Macroeconomic instability and business exit: Determinants of failures and acquisitions of UK Firms. *Economica,* 76, 108–31.

Birch, D. L. 1987. *Job Creation in America*. New York, Free Press.

Blackburn, R. A. 2003. *Intellectual Property and Innovation Management in Small Firms*. London, Routledge.

Blanchflower, D. G. and Oswald, A. J. 1998. What makes an entrepreneur? *Journal of Labour Economics,* 16, 26–60.

Bleaney, M. and Wakelin, K. 2002. Efficiency, innovation and exports. *Oxford Bulletin of Economics and Statistics,* 64, 3–15.

Blind, K. and Jumgmittag, A. 2004. Foreign direct investment, imports and innovations in the service industry. *Review of Industrial Organisation,* 25, 205–27.

Bolton, W. K. and Thompson, J. L. 2000. *Entrepreneurs: Talent, temperament, technique.* London, Butterworth-Heinemann.

Borger, J. 2007. Organised crime: The $2 trillion threat to the world's security. *The Guardian,* 12 September.

Bosma, N. and Levie, J. 2010. Global report. *Global Entrepreneurship Monitor.*

Bottazzi, G., Cefis, E. and Dosi, G. 2002. Corporate growth and industrial structures: Some evidence from the Italian manufacturing industry. *Industrial and Corporate Change,* 11, 705–23.

Bottazzi, G., Coad, A., Jacoby, N. and Secchi, A. 2011. Corporate growth and industrial dynamics: Evidence from French manufacturing. *Applied Economics,* 43, 103–16.

Braczyk, H. J., Cooke, P. and Heidenreich, M. 1998. *Regional Innovation Systems: The role of governance in a globalised world*. London and Pennsylvania, UCL Press.

Bramwell, A. and Wolfe, D. A. 2008. Universities and regional economic development: The entrepreneurial University of Waterloo. *Research Policy,* 37, 1175–87.

Bramwell, A., Nelles, J. and Wolfe, D. A. 2008. Knowledge, innovation and institutions: Global and local dimensions of the ICT Cluster in Waterloo, Canada. *Regional Studies,* 42, 105–22.

Bresnahan, T. F. and Gambardella, A. 2004. *Silicon Valley and its Imitators*. Cambridge, Cambridge University Press.

Bruton, G. D., Ahlstrom, D. and Puky, T. 2009. Institutional differences and the development of entrepreneurial ventures: A comparison of the venture capital industries in Latin America and Asia. *Journal of International Business Studies,* 40, 762–78.

Bruton, G. D., Ahlstrom, D. and Li, H. L. 2010. Institutional theory and entrepreneurship: Where are we now and where do we need to move in the future? *Entrepreneurship Theory and Practice,* 34, 421–40.

Buen, J. 2006. Danish and Norwegian wind industry: The relationship between policy instruments, innovation and diffusion. *Energy Policy,* 34, 3887–97.

Buys, A. J. and Mbewana, P. N. 2007. Key success factors for business incubation in South Africa: The Godisa case study. *South African Journal of Science,* 103, 356–8.

Cainelli, G., Rinaldo, E. and Savona, M. 2004. The impact of innovation on economic performance in services. *Service Industries Journal,* 24, 116–30.

Cainelli, G., Evangelista, R. and Savona, M. 2006. Innovation and economic performance in services: A firm-level analysis. *Cambridge Journal of Economics,* 30, 435–58.

Caliendo, M. and Kritikos, A. 2008. Start-ups by the unemployed: Characteristics, survival and direct employment effects. *Small Business Economics,* 35, 71–92.

Capelleras, J.-L., Mole, K. F., Greene, F. J. and Storey, D. J. 2008. Do more heavily regulated economies have poorer performing new ventures? Evidence from Britain and Spain. *Journal of International Business Studies,* 39, 688–704.

Carter, S. and Marlow, S. (2007), Female entrepreneurship: Empirical evidence and theoretical perspectives in Carter, N., Henry, C. and O'Cinneide, B. (eds) *Promoting Female Entrepreneurs: Implications for Education, Training and Policy.* London, Routledge.

CAWTAR/IFC 2007. *Women Entrepreneurs in the Middle East and North Africa: Characteristics, contributions and challenges.* Tunis, Centre of Arab Women for Training and Research/International Finance Corporation.

Chell, E. 2001. *Entrepreneurship: Globalization, innovation and development.* London, Thomson Learning.

Chizema, A. and Buck, T. 2006. Neo-institutional theory and institutional change: Towards empirical tests on the 'Americanization' of German executive pay. *International Business Review,* 15, 488–504.

Churchill, N. 2000. The six phases of company growth in Birley, S. and Muzyka, D. F. (eds) *Mastering Entrepreneurship: The complete MBA companion in entrepreneurship.* London, Prentice Hall.

Clinard, M. B. and Quinney, R. 1967. *Criminal Behavior Systems: A typology.* New York, Holt, Rinehart and Winston.

Coleman, S. 2004. The liability of newness and small firm access to debt capital: Is there a link?. Washington DC, *Annual Conference of the Academy of Entrepreneurial Finance.*

—— 2007. The role of human and financial capital in the profitability and growth of women-owned small firms. *Journal of Small Business Management,* 45, 303–19.

Colombier, N. and Masclet, D. 2008. Intergenerational correlation in self employment: Some further evidence from French ECHP data. *Small Business Economics,* 30, 423–37.

Cooke, P. 2004. The regional innovation system in Wales – Evolution or eclipse? in Cooke, P., Heidenreich, M. and Braczyk H. J., (eds) *Regional Innovation Systems.* London, Routledge.

Cooke, P. and Leydesdorff, L. 2006. Regional development in the knowledge-based economy: The construction of advantage. *Journal of Technology Transfer,* 31, 5–15.

Cooke, P., Uranga, G. and Etxebarria, G. 1997. Regional innovation systems: Institutional and organisational dimensions. *Research Policy,* 26, 475–91.

Crepon, A., Hughes, A., Lee, P. and Mairesse, J. 1998. Research, innovation and productivity: An econometric analysis at the firm level. *Economics of Innovation and New Technology,* 7, 115–58.

Cressy, R. 2006. Determinants of small firm growth and survival in Casson, M., Yeung, B., Basu, A. and Wadeson, N. (eds) *Oxford Handbook of Entrepreneurship.* Oxford, Oxford University Press.

Curran, J. 1986. *Bolton 15 Years On: A review and analysis of small business research in Britain 1971–86.* London, Small Business Research Trust.

De Clercq, D. and Arenius, P. 2006. The role of knowledge in business start-up activity. *International Small Business Journal,* 24, 339–58.

De Vries, K. 1977. The entrepreneurial personality: A person at the crossroad. *Journal of Management Studies,* 1, 34–57.

Djankov, S., Lieberman, I., Mukherjee, J. and Nenova, T. 2002a. *Going Informal: Benefits and costs.* Washington DC, World Bank.

Djankov, S., La Porta, R., Lopez-De-Silanes, F. and Shleifer, A. 2002b. The regulation of entry. *Quarterly Journal of Economics,* 117, 1–37.

Djankov, S., Qian, Y., Roland, G. and Zhuravskaya, E. 2006. Entrepreneurship in Russia and China compared. *Journal of the European Economic Association,* 4, 352–65.

Dolfsma, W. and Leydesdorff, L. 2009. Lock-in and break-out from technological trajectories: Modeling and policy implications. *Technological Forecasting and Social Change,* 76, 932–41.

Drucker, P. F. 1993. *Innovation and Entrepreneurship.* New York, Harper Business.

Druilhe, C. and Garnsey, E. 2003. Do academic spin-outs differ and does it matter? University of Cambridge, *Centre for Technology Management Working Paper, 2003/02.*

Duan, H., Han, X. and Hongbo, Y. 2009. An analysis of causes for SMEs financing difficulty. *International Journal of Business and Management,* 4, 73–5.

Duff, A. 1994. *Best Practice in Business Incubator Management.* Booragoon, WA, Australia, AUSTEP Strategic Partnering Pty.

Edler, J. and Georghiou, L. 2007. Public procurement and innovation – Resurrecting the demand side. *Research Policy,* 36, 949–63.

Efrat, K. and Shoham, A. 2011. Environmental characteristics and technological capabilities' interaction in high-technology born global firms. *European Journal of International Management,* 5, 271–84.

Elfring, T. and Hulsink, W. 2003. Networks in entrepreneurship: The case of high-technology firms. *Small Business Economics,* 21, 409–22.

Eraydin, A., Tasan-Kok, T. and Vranken, J. 2010. Diversity matters: Immigrant entrepreneurship and contribution of different forms of social integration in economic performance of cities. *European Planning Studies,* 18, 521–43.

Ernst, D. and Kim, L. 2002. Global production networks, knowledge diffusion and local capability formation. *Research Policy,* 31, 1417–30.

Essers, C. and Benschop, Y. 2009. Muslim businesswomen doing boundary work: The negotiation of Islam, gender and ethnicity within entrepreneurial contexts. *Human Relations,* 62, 403–23.

EU 2004. *Management of Intellectual Property in Publicly-Funded Research Organisations: Towards European Guidelines.* Luxembourg, European Commission.

Fiol, M. 2001. Revisiting an identity-based view of sustainable competitive advantage. *Journal of Management,* 6, 691–9.

Flodman-Becker, K. 2004. *The Informal Economy.* Stockholm, SIDA.

Florida, R. 2005. *Cities and the Creative Class.* Abingdon, Routledge.

Floyd, K. H. 2010. *Somalia's Stability and Security Situation in Review.* International Centre for Political Violence and Terrorism Research, S. Rajartnam School of International Studies.

Fraser, S. 2005. *Finance for Small and Medium Sized Enterprises – A report on the 2004 UK survey of SME finances.* University of Warwick, Centre for Small and Medium Enterprises.

Fraser, S., Greene, F. J. and Mole, K. F. 2007. Systematic biases in self-reported data: The role of anchoring and impression management. *British Journal of Management,* 18, 192–208.

Fritsch, M. and Mueller, P. 2004. Effects of new business formation on regional development over time. *Regional Studies,* 38, 961–75.

Fuchs, G. and Shapira, P. 2005. *Rethinking Regional Innovation: Path dependency or regional breakthrough.* New York, Springer.

Fujita, M. and Thisse, J. F. 2002. *Economics of Agglomeration: Cities, industrial location and regional growth.* Cambridge, Cambridge University Press.

GEM 2007. *2007 Global Report on High Growth Entrepreneurship.* Available at: http://www.gemconsortium.org/docs

GEM 2009. *2009 Global Report.* Available at: http://www.genconsortium.org/docs.

GEM 2010. *Global Entrepreneurship Monitor: 2010 Global Report.* Available at: http://www.gemconsortium.org/docs

Geroski, P., Machin, S. and Van Reenen, J. 1993. The profitability of innovating firms. *Rand Journal of Economics,* 24, 198–211.

Gibrat, R. 1931. *Les Inegalites Economiques. Applications: Aux Inegalites des Richesses, a la Concentration des Entreprises, Aux Populations des Villes, Aux Statistiques des Familles, etc., d'une Loi Nouvelle: La Loi de l'Effect Proportionnel.* Paris, Sirey.

Goedhuys, M. and Sleuwaegen, L. 2010. High-growth entrepreneurial firms in Africa: A quantile regression approach. *Small Business Economics,* 34, 31–51.

Gorton, M., Ignat, G. and White, J. 2004. The evolution of post-Soviet labour processes: A case study of the hollowing out of paternalism in Moldova. *International Journal of Human Resource Management,* 15, 1249–61.

Gorton, M., White, J. and Dumitrashko, M. 2005. Applying the clinical inquiry approach to understand and facilitate enterprise restructuring in transitional economies: A case study from the Moldovan wine industry. *Systemic Practice and Action Research,* 18, 35–52.

Gorton, M., Dumitrashko, M. and White, J. 2006. Overcoming supply chain failure in the agri-food sector: A case study from Moldova. *Food Policy,* 31, 90–103.

Green, A., Mostafa, T. and Preston, J. 2010. *The Chimera of Competitiveness: Varieties of capitalism and the economic crisis.* London, Centre for Learning and Life Chances in Knowledge Economies and Societies.

Greiner, L. E. 1972. Evolution and revolution as organisations grow. *Harvard Business Review,* 50, 37–46.

Groh, A. P. and von Liechtenstein, H. 2009. How attractive is central Eastern Europe for risk capital investors? *Journal of International Money and Finance,* 28, 625–47.

Guellec, D. and van Pottelsberghe, B. 2001. *The Effectiveness of Public R&D Policies in OECD Countries.* Paris, Organisation for Economic Co-operation and Development.

—— 2004. From R&D to productivity growth: Do the institutional settings and the source of funds matter? *Oxford Bulletin of Economics and Statistics,* 66, 353–78.

Hanks, S. H., Watson, C. J., Jasen, E. and Chandler, G. N. 1993. Tightening the life-cycle construct: A taxonomic study of growth stage configurations in high-technology organisations. *Entrepreneurship Theory and Practice,* 18, 5–29.

Hansen, M. T. and Birkinshaw, J. 2007. The innovation value chain. *Harvard Business Review,* June, 121–30.

Hanson, S. 2009. Changing places through women's entrepreneurship. *Economic Geography,* 85, 245–67.

Harrison, J. R. 2004. Models of growth in organizational ecology: A simulation assessment. *Industrial and Corporate Change,* 13, 243–61.

Hayter, C. S. 2011. In search of the profit-maximizing actor: Motivations and definitions of success from nascent academic entrepreneurs. *Journal of Technology Transfer,* 36, 340–52.

Henderson, J., Dicken, P., Hess, M., Coe, N. and Yeung, H. Y. C. 2002. Global production networks and the analysis of economic development. *Review of International Political Economy,* 9, 436–64.

Henrekson, M. and Johansson, D. 2010. Gazelles as job creators: A survey and interpretation of the evidence. *Small Business Economics,* 35, 227–44.

Hewitt-Dundas, N. 2006. Resource and capability constraints to innovation in small and large plants. *Small Business Economics,* 26, 257–77.

Hoang, H. and Antoncic, B. 2003. Network-based research in entrepreneurship – A critical review. *Journal of Business Venturing,* 18, 165–87.

Hogan, T. and Hutson, E. 2004. *Is There a High Technology Pecking Order? An investigation of the capital structure of NTBFs in the Irish software sector.* University College Dublin, Working Paper.

Hornsby, R. and Hobbs, D. 2007. A zone of ambiguity – The political economy of cigarette bootlegging. *British Journal of Criminology,* 47, 551–71.

Hovorka, A. 2006. The #1 ladies' poultry farm: A feminist political ecology of urban agriculture in Botswana. *Gender, Place, and Culture,* 13, 207–25.

Howarth, C. A. 2001. Small firms' demand for finance. *International Small Business Journal,* 19, 78–86.

IFF Research Ltd 2008. *BERR Household Survey of Entrepreneurship 2007.* London, Department for Business, Enterprise and Regulatory Reform.

International Association of Islamic Banks. 1995. *Directory of Islamic Banks and Financial Institutions.* Jeddah, IAIB.

Isa, K. D. and Terungwa, A. 2011. An empirical evaluation of small and medium enterprises equity investment scheme in Nigeria. *International Conference on Economics and Finance Research.* Singapore, IACSIT Press.

Johnson, P. 2005. Targeting firm births and economic regeneration in a lagging region. *Small Business Economics,* 24, 451–64.

Johnson, W. 2009. So what or so everything? Bringing behavior genetics to entrepreneurship research. *Journal of Business Venturing,* 24, 23–6.

Jones, M. V., Coviello, N. and Tang, Y. K. 2011. International entrepreneurship research (1989–2009): A domain ontology and thematic analysis. *Journal of Business Venturing,* 26, 632–59.

Joshi, K., Amoranto, G. and Hasan, R. 2011. Informal sector enterprises: Some measurement issues. *Review of Income and Wealth,* 57, S143–S165.

Jovanic, B. 1982. Selection and the evolution of industry. *Econometrica,* 50, 649–70.

Kang, J. W. and Heshmati, A. 2008. Effect of credit guarantee policy on survival and performance of SMEs in Republic of Korea. *Small Business Economics,* 31, 445–62.

Karupiah, P. 2010. *Gender, Aspiration and Choice to Become an Entrepreneur among Malaysian Graduates.* Liverpool, World Acad Union-World Acad Press.

Kautonen, T., Luoto, S. and Tornikoski, E. T. 2010. Influence of work history on entrepreneurial intentions in 'prime age' and 'third age': A preliminary study. *International Small Business Journal,* 28, 583–601.

Kholis, N. 2008. Murabahah mode of financing for micro and medium sized enterprises: A case study of Baitul Mal Wattamwil (BMT), Yogyakarta, Indonesia in Obaidullah, M. and Latiff, H. S. H. A. (eds) *Islamic Finance for Micro and Medium Enterprises.* Darussalam, Centre for Islamic Banking, Finance and Management.

Kihlstrom, R. E. and Laffont, J. J. 1979. A general equilibrium entrepreneurial theory of firm formation based on risk aversion. *Journal of Political Economy,* 87, 719–48.

Knight, F. 1921. *Risk, Uncertainty and Profit.* Boston MA, Hart, Schaffner & Marx.

Kon, Y. and Storey, D. J. 2003. A theory of discouraged borrowers. *Small Business Economics,* 21, 37–49.

Koski, H., Rouvinen, P. and Ylä-Antilla, P. 2002. ICT Clusters in Europe – The great central banana and the small Nordic potato. *Information Economics and Policy,* 14, 145–65.

Kostova, T. 1999. Transnational transfer of strategic organizational practices: A contextual perspective. *Academy of Management Review,* 24, 308–24.

Lachenmaier, S. and Wobmann, L. 2006. Does innovation cause exports? Evidence from exogenous innovation impulses and obstacles using German micro data. *Oxford Economic Papers,* 58, 317–50.

Landesco, J. 1929. *Organized Crime in Chicago.* Chicago, Illinois Association for Criminal Justice, Illinois Crime Survey.

Langan-Fox, J. 2005. Analysing achievement, motivation and leadership in women entrepreneurs – A new integration in Fielden, S. L. and Davidson, M. J. (eds) *International Handbook of Women and Small Business Entrepreneurship.* Cheltenham, Edward Elgar.

Lanjouw, J. O. and Schankerman, M. 2004. Protecting intellectual property rights: Are small firms handicapped? *Journal of Law and Economics,* 48, 1, 45–74.

Leiponen, A. 2000. Competencies, innovation and profitability of firms. *Economics of Innovation and New Technology,* 9, 1–24.

Lerner, M., Brush, C. and Hisrich, R. 1997. Israeli women entrepreneurs: An examination of factors affecting performance. *Journal of Business Venturing,* 12, 315–39.

Levitsky, J. and Prasad, R. N. 1989. Credit Guarantee Schemes for Small and Medium Enterprises. New York, *World Bank Technical Paper No 58.*

Liao, J. and Welsch, H. 2008. Patterns of venture gestation process: Exploring the differences between tech and non-tech nascent entrepreneurs. *Journal of High Technology Management Research,* 19, 103–13

Lockett, A., Wright, M. and Franklin, S. 2003. Technology transfer and universities' spin out strategies. *Small Business Economics,* 20, 2, 185–200.

Loof, H. and Heshmati, A. 2001. *On the Relationship between Innovation and Performance: A sensitivity analysis.* Stockholm, Stockholm School of Economics.

—— 2002. Knowledge capital and performance heterogeneity: A firm level innovation study. *International Journal of Production Economics,* 76, 61–85.

Love, J. H., Hewitt-Dundas, N. and Roper, S. 2010. Service innovation, embeddedness and business performance. *Regional Studies,* 44, 983–1004

Lu, J. Y. and Tao, Z. G. 2010. Determinants of entrepreneurial activities in China. *Journal of Business Venturing,* 25, 261–73.

Macpherson, A. and Holt, R. 2007. Knowledge, learning and small firm growth: A systematic review of the evidence. *Research Policy,* 36, 172–92.

Manigart, S. and Struyf, C. 1997. Financing high technology startups in Belgium: An explorative study. *Small Business Economics,* 9, 125–35.

Mansfield, E. 1986. The R&D tax credit and other technology policy issues. *American Economic Review (Papers and Proceedings),* 76, 1190–4.

McClelland, D. C. 1961. *The Achieving Society.* New York, Free Press.

McDade, B. E. and Spring, A. 2005. The 'new generation of African entrepreneurs': Networking to change the climate for business and private sector-led development. *Entrepreneurship and Regional Development,* 17, 17–42.

McMahon, R. G. P. 2001. Deriving an empirical development taxonomy for manufacturing SMEs using data from Australia's Business Longitudinal Survey. *Small Business Economics,* 17, 197–212.

Metcalfe, S. 1997. *Technology Systems and Technology Policy in an Evolutionary Framework.* Cambridge, Cambridge University Press.

Meurs, M., Welter, F., Smallbone, D. and Isakova, N. 2008. Enterprising women in transition economies. *Feminist Economics,* 14, 150–4.

Mitton, D. G. 1989. The compleat entrepreneur. *Entrepreneurship, Theory and Practice,* 13, 9–19.

Mole, K., Hart, M., Roper, S. and Saal, S. 2008a. Assessing the effectiveness of business support services in England: Evidence from a theory based evaluation. *International Small Business Journal,* 27, 557–82.

Mole, K. F., Hart, M., Roper, S. and Saal, D. 2008b. Differential gains from business link support and advice: A treatment effects approach. *Environment and Planning C,* 26, 316–34.

Morris, M. H., Miyasaki, N. N., Watters, C. E. and Coombes, S. M. 2006. The dilemma of growth: Understanding venture size choices of women entrepreneurs. *Journal of Small Business Management,* 44, 221–44.

Mowery, D., Nelson, R., Sampat, B. and Ziedonis, A. 2004. *Ivory Tower and Industrial Innovation: University-industry technology transfer before and after the Bayh-Dole Act.* Palo Alto CA, Stanford University Press.

Mutula, S. M. and Van Brakel, P. 2007. ICT skills readiness for the emerging global digital economy among small businesses in developing countries: Case study of Botswana. *Library Hi Tech,* 25, 231–45.

Ndonzuau, F. N., Pirnay, F. and Surlemont, B. 2002. A stage model of academic spin-off creation. *Technovation,* 22, 281–9.

Nelson, R. R. 1993. *National Systems of Innovation: A comparative study.* Oxford, Oxford University Press.

NESTA 2008. *Developing Entrepreneurial Graduates – Putting entrepreneurship at the centre of higher education.* London, CIHE-NCGE-NESTA.

Ngowi, A. B., Iwisi, D. S. and Mushi, R. J. 2002. Competitive strategy in a context of low financial resources. *Building Research and Information,* 30, 205–11.

Nicholson, L. and Anderson, A. R. 2005. News and nuances of the entrepreneurial myth and metaphor: Linguistic games in entrepreneurial sense-making and sense-giving. *Entrepreneurship, Theory and Practice,* 29, 153–73.

Nicolaou, N. and Shane, S. 2010. Entrepreneurship and occupational choice: Genetic and environmental influences. *Journal of Economic Behavior and Organization,* 76, 3–14.

Nicolaou, N., Shane, S., Cherkas, L., Hunkin, J. and Spector, T. D. 2008. Is the tendency to engage in entrepreneurship genetic? *Management Science,* 54, 167–79.

Nicolaou, N., Shane, S., Cherkas, L. and Spector, T. D. 2009. Opportunity recognition and the tendency to be an entrepreneur: A bivariate genetics perspective. *Organizational Behavior and Human Decision Processes,* 110, 108–17.

Norberg-Bohm, V. 2000. Creating incentives for environmentally enhancing technological change: Lessons from 30 years of US energy technology policy. *Technological Forecasting and Social Change,* 65, 125–48.

North, D. C. 1990. *Institutions, Institutional Change and Economic Performance.* Cambridge, Cambridge University Press.

Obaidullah, M. and Latiff, H. S. H. A. 2008. *Islamic Finance for Micro and Medium Enterprises.* Universiti Brunei Darussalam.

OECD 2008a. *Compendium of Patent Statistics.* Paris, Organisation for Economic Co-operation and Development.

—— 2008b. Measuring entrepreneurship – A digest of indicators. *OECD-Eurostat EEIP Programme.*

Olson, E. M., Walker, O. C. and Ruekert, R. W. 1995. Organising for effective new product development – The moderating role of product innovativeness. *Journal of Marketing,* 59, 48–62.

Parker, S. C., Storey, D. J. and van Witteloostuijn, A. 2010. What happens to gazelles? The importance of dynamic management strategy. *Small Business Economics,* 35, 203–26.

Parnell, J. A. and Dent, E. B. 2009. The role of luck in the strategy–performance relationship. *Management Decision,* 47, 1000–21.

Pearson, G. and Hobbs, D. 2003. King pin? A case study of a middle market drug broker. *Howard Journal,* 42, 335–47.

Perez, Y. and Ramos-Real, F. J. 2009. The public promotion of wind energy in Spain from the transaction costs perspective 1986–2007. *Renewable & Sustainable Energy Reviews,* 13, 1058–66.

Pike, A., Rodríguez-Pose, A. and Tomaney, J. 2006. *Local and Regional Development.* London, Routledge.

Pillai, P. S. and Amma, K. S. 2005. Women small business owners in India in Fielden, S. L. and Davidson, M. J. (eds) *International Handbook of Women and Small Business Entrepreneurship.* Cheltenham, Edward Elgar.

Pinger, P. 2010. Come back or stay? Spend here or there? Return and remittances: The case of Moldova. *International Migration,* 48, 142–73.

Piva, M. and Vivarelli, M. 2007. Is demand-pulled innovation equally important in different groups of firms? *Cambridge Journal of Economics,* 31, 691–710.

Plattner, I. E., Lechaena, M., Mmolawa, W. and Mzingwane, B. 2009. Are university students psychologically ready for entrepreneurship? A Botswana study. *African Journal of Business Management,* 3, 305–10.

Porter, M. E. 1998. Clusters and the new economics of competition. *Harvard Business Review,* 76(6), 77–90.

Potter, J. and Storey, D. 2007. *OECD Framework for the Evaluation of SME and Entrepreneurship Policy and Programmes.* Paris, Organisation for Economic Co-operation and Development.

Puffer, S. M., McCarthy, D. J. and Boisot, M. 2010. Entrepreneurship in Russia and China: The impact of formal institutional voids. *Entrepreneurship Theory and Practice,* 34, 441–67.

Radu, M. and Redien-Collot, R. 2008. The social representation of entrepreneurs in the French press – Desirable and feasible models? *International Small Business Journal,* 26, 259–98.

Rauch, A. and Frese, M. 2007. Let's put the person back into entrepreneurship research: A meta-analysis on the relationship between business owners' personality traits, business creation, and success. *European Journal of Work and Organizational Psychology,* 16, 353–85.

Reddy, P. 1997. New trends in globalisation of corporate R&D and implications for innovation capability in host countries: A survey from India. *World Development,* 25, 1821–38.

Roberts, E. B. 1991. *Entrepreneurs in High Technology – Lessons from MIT and beyond.* Oxford, Oxford University Press.

Robinson, M. J. and Cotterell, T. J. 2007. Investment patterns of informal investors in the Alberta private equity market. *Journal of Small Business Management,* 45, 47–67.

Robson, G. B. 1996. Unravelling the facts about job generation. *Small Business Economics,* 8, 409–17.

Robson, P. J. A., Haugh, H. M. and Obeng, B. A. 2009. Entrepreneurship and innovation in Ghana: Enterprising Africa. *Small Business Economics,* 32, 331–50.

Roper, S. 1999. Modelling small business growth and profitability. *Small Business Economics,* 13, 235–52.

Roper, S. and Hewitt-Dundas, N. 2001. Grant assistance and small firm development in Northern Ireland and the Republic of Ireland. *Scottish Journal of Political Economy,* 48, 99–117.

Roper, S. and Love, J. H. 2002. Innovation and export performance: Evidence from UK and German manufacturing plants. *Research Policy,* 31, 1087–1102.

Roper, S. and Scott, J. 2009. Perceived financial barriers and the start-up decision: An econometric analysis of gender differences using GEM data. *International Small Business Journal,* 2, 149–71.

Roper, S., Love, J. H., Cooke, P. and Clifton, N. 2006. *The Scottish Innovation Systems: Actors, roles and actions.* Report for the Scottish Executive. Available at http://www.scotland.gov.uk/Resource/Doc/89713/0021562.pdf

Roper, S., Du, J. and Love, J. H. 2008. Modelling the innovation value chain. *Research Policy,* 37, 961–77.

Rosenbusch, N., Rauch, A., Parker, S. C. and Unger, J. M. 2009. *Human Capital, Gender and Entrepreneurial Success: Empirical evidence from China and Germany.*

Washington DC, Paper presented at the World Bank Conference, 'Female Entrepreneurship: Constraints and opportunities'.

Rosenbusch, N., Brinckmann, J. and Bausch, A. 2011. Is innovation always beneficial? A meta-analysis of the relationship between innovation and performance in SMEs. *Journal of Business Venturing,* 26, 441–57.

Rotter, J. B. 1966. Generalized expectancies for internal versus external control of reinforcement. *Psychological Monographs,* 80, 1–2.

Sarasola, J. M. and Laspiur, J. D. 2006. *Mediapila Pais – A case study of social enterprise activities.* Santiago, Chile, 2006 Latin American Social Enterprise Symposium.

Saxenian, A. 1996. *Regional Advantage: Culture and competition in Silicon Valley and Route 128.* Harvard, Mass., Harvard University Press.

Schumpeter, J. A. 1912. *Theorie der wirtschaftlichen Entwicklung.* Leipzig, Duncker and Humblo.

Scott, J. M. and Irwin, D. 2009. Discouraged advisees? The influence of gender, ethnicity, and education in the use of advice and finance by UK SMEs. *Environment and Planning C: Government and Policy,* 27, 230–45.

Sine, W. D. and Lee, B. H. 2009. Tilting at windmills? The environmental movement and the emergence of the US wind energy sector. *Administrative Science Quarterly,* 54, 123–55.

Smith, D. J. 1980. Paragons, pariahs and pirates: A spectrum based theory of enterprise. *Crime and Delinquency,* 26, 358–86.

Solleiro, J. L., Paniagua, J. and Castanon, R. 2006. Managing of technology in Mexican firms: The case of Instituto Bioclon. *2006 IEEE Conference on Management of Innovation and Technology,* 1075–9.

Sorensen, B. M. 2008. 'Behold, I am making all things new': The entrepreneur as savior in the age of creativity. *Scandinavian Journal of Management,* 24, 85–93.

Stenning, A., Smith, A., Rochovska, A. and Swiatek, D. 2010. Credit, debt, and everyday financial practices: Low-income households in two postsocialist cities. *Economic Geography,* 86, 119–45.

Sterlacchini, A. 1999. Do innovative activities matter to small firms in non-R&D-intensive industries? An application to export performance. *Research Policy,* 28, 819–32.

Storey, D. J. 1994. *Understanding the Small Business Sector.* London, Routledge.

—— 2011. Optimism and chance: The elephants in the entrepreneurship room. *International Small Business Journal,* 29, 303–21.

Storey, D. J. and Johnson, S. 1986. Job generation in Britain: A review of recent studies. *International Small Business Journal,* 4, 29–46.

Stuart, T. and Sorenson, O. 2003. The geography of opportunity: Spatial heterogeneity in founding rates and the performance of biotechnology firms. *Research Policy,* 32, 229–53.

Suurs, R. A. A., Hekkert, M. P., Kieboom, S. and Smits, R. 2010. Understanding the formative stage of technological innovation system development: The case of natural gas as an automotive fuel. *Energy Policy,* 38, 419–31.

Taniguchi, H. 2002. Determinants of women's entry into self-employment. *Social Science Quarterly,* 83, 875–93.

Townsend, D. M., Busenitz, L. W. and Arthurs, J. D. 2010. To start or not to start: Outcome and ability expectations in the decision to start a new venture. *Journal of Business Venturing,* 25, 192–202.

Tracey, P. 2011. Institutional approaches to entrepreneurship in Mole, K. (ed.) *Perspectives in Entrepreneurship: A critical approach.* Basingstoke, Palgrave Macmillan.

Tsai, W. H. and Kuo, H. C. 2011. Entrepreneurship policy evaluation and decision analysis for SMEs. *Expert Systems with Applications,* 38, 8343–51.

Usai, S. 2011. The geography of inventive activity in OECD regions. *Regional Studies,* 45, 711–31.

Vaillant, Y. and Lafuente, E. 2007. Do different institutional frameworks condition the influence of local fear of failure and entrepreneurial examples over entrepreneurial activity? *Entrepreneurship and Regional Development,* 19, 313–37.

Van de Ven, A. H. and Engleman, R. M. 2004. Event and outcome driven explanations of entrepreneurship. *Journal of Business Venturing,* 19, 343–58.

van der Boon, M. 2005. Women into enterprise – A European and international perspective in Fielden, S. L. and Davidson, M. J. (eds) *International Handbook of Women and Small Business Entrepreneurship.* Cheltenham, Edward Elgar.

Vanacker, T. R. and Manigart, S. 2010. Pecking order and debt capacity considerations for high-growth companies seeking financing. *Small Business Economics,* 35, 53–69.

Visser, H. 2009. *Islamic Finance: Principles and practice.* Cheltenham, Edward Elgar.

Von Stamm, B. 2003. *Innovation, Creativity and Design.* Chichester, John Wiley.

Vossen, R. W. 1998. Relative strengths and weaknesses of small firms in innovation. *International Small Business Journal,* 16, 88–95.

Wakelin, K. 1998. Innovation and export behaviour at the firm level. *Research Policy,* 26, 829–41.

Welter, F. and Smallbone, D. 2011. Institutional perspectives on entrepreneurial behavior in challenging environments. *Journal of Small Business Management,* 49, 107–25.

Wiklund, J., Patzelt, H. and Shepherd, D. A. 2009. Building an integrative model of small business growth. *Small Business Economics,* 32, 351–74.

Willis, J. 2003. New generation drinking: The uncertain boundaries of criminal enterprise in modern Kenya. *African Affairs,* 102, 241–60.

Wright, M., Lockett, A., Clarysse, B. and Binks, M. 2006. University spin-out companies and venture capital. *Research Policy,* 35, 481–501.

Xiao, L. 2011. Financing high-tech SMEs in China: A three-stage model of business development. *Entrepreneurship and Regional Development,* 23, 217–34.

Ylinenpaa, H. 2009. Entrepreneurship and innovation systems: Towards a development of the ERIS/IRIS concept. *European Planning Studies,* 17, 1153–70.

Zhang, Z., Zyphur, M. J., Narayanan, J., Arvey, R. D., Chaturvedi, S., Avolio, B. J., Lichtenstein, P. and Larsson, G. 2009. The genetic basis of entrepreneurship: Effects of gender and personality. *Organizational Behavior and Human Decision Processes,* 110, 93–107.

Zhao, X. Y., Frese, M. and Giardini, A. 2010. Business owners' network size and business growth in China: The role of comprehensive social competency. *Entrepreneurship and Regional Development,* 22, 675–705.

Index

Page numbers in *italics* represent tables. Page numbers in **bold** represent figures. Page numbers followed by b represent box.

Index of countries

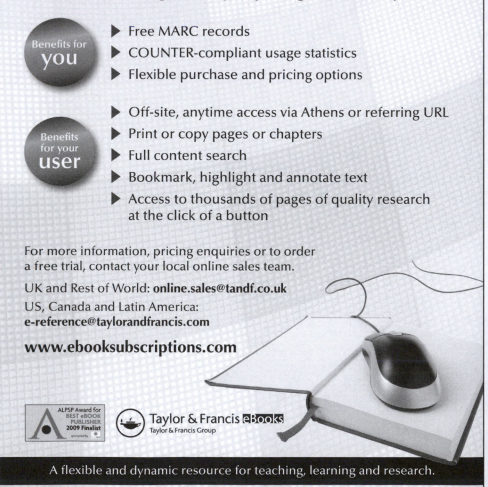